M000318047

IMMIGRATION
The
Economic Case

IMMIGRATION
The
Economic Case

Diane Francis

KEY PORTER BOOKS

Copyright © 2002 by Diane Francis

All rights reserved. No part of this work covered by the copyrights hereon may be reproduced or used in any form or by any means—graphic, electronic or mechanical, including photo-copying, recording, taping or information storage and retrieval systems—without the prior written permission of the publisher, or in the case of photocopying or other reprographic copying, a license from the Canadian Copyright Licensing Agency.

National Library of Canada Cataloguing in Publication Data

Francis, Diane, 1946–

    Immigration: the economic case/Diane Francis

Includes index.
ISBN 1-55263-532-5

    1. Canada—Emigration and immigration—Economic aspects. 2. Canada—Emigration and immigration—Government policy. 3. Canada—Economic conditions—1991–. I. Title.

JV7225.F73 2002   330.971'0648   C2002-903417-5

THE CANADA COUNCIL | LE CONSEIL DES ARTS
FOR THE ARTS | DU CANADA
SINCE 1957 | DEPUIS 1957

ONTARIO ARTS COUNCIL
CONSEIL DES ARTS DE L'ONTARIO

The publisher gratefully acknowledges the support of the Canada Council for the Arts and the Ontario Arts Council for its publishing program.

We acknowledge the financial support of the Government of Canada through the Book Publishing Industry Development Program (BPIDP) for our publishing activities.

Key Porter Books Limited
70 The Esplanade
Toronto, Ontario
Canada M5E 1R2

www.keyporter.com

Text design: Peter Maher
Electronic formatting: Heidy Lawrance Associates
Printed and bound in Canada

02 03 04 05 06 07 6 5 4 3 2 1

To Eric and Julie

Table of Contents

Introduction

I grew up in the United States and immigrated to Canada in 1966 with a British husband who had a U.S. Green Card. The Vietnam War was heating up, and it was only a matter of time before he would be drafted by the U.S. military. Once conscripted, he would have had a choice of serving in the military or leaving. So we decided to immigrate to Australia. But after making inquiries, I learned that Australia was America's ally in the Vietnam War and also drafted young male immigrants. Because my husband refused to consider returning to Britain, we zeroed in on Plan B, which was to immigrate to Canada. It was cold, but it was English-speaking, prosperous, and, most importantly, not involved in Vietnam. We applied, were accepted as immigrants, and drove to Toronto several months later, in a used car filled with clothes, pots, and pans. We did not know anyone, but there were plenty of jobs and lots of opportunities. We were successful.

I eventually became a business writer and, as such, have realized that Canada's decision to let us come here was not about handing out charity or about providing pacifist comfort to draft dodgers. We were allowed in because we were young, healthy, educated, and had skills that were in demand. That's what immigration in Canada, until only recently, has mostly been about. Recruitment, not charity.

We had made an appointment at the Canadian consulate in Chicago and were interviewed twice by an immigration officer. We were tested for literacy and intelligence, had medical examinations, and produced references about our employability, education credentials, and financial status. There was a point system against which we were measured. More points for English or French language skills. More points for a university degree or a professional skill and so on. We were told that there was still room for us that particular year, based on labor market needs, unemployment rates, and other market conditions. The immigration officer noted that if we did not get in that year we could pay our $150 again and re-apply. Fortunately, only a few weeks later we got the good news. We had received "landed immigrant" status and were given six months to exercise the privilege.

Looking back, the care and research that led to our approval was protection for us as well as for our adopted country. When we arrived, our skills were in demand and jobs in our fields (I was a legal secretary and he was a commercial artist) were plentiful. We lived in a cheap, comfortable rooming house with other immigrants in Toronto who were from the U.S. or Europe. And all of us benefited from the same experience.

This book, and a body of work that I have produced over several years, is about the fact that Canada's employment-centered immigration policy began to be eroded in the mid-1980s at the same time as the numbers of applicants skyrocketed. Between 1986 and 2000, a period of 15 calendar years, 3,035,615 persons were let into this country, constituting one-fifth of the entire 15,184,953 who arrived between 1851 and 2000. This hasn't been an influx. It has been a deluge of people equivalent, in size, to the population of Regina each year, irrespective of Canada's economic conditions or the immigrants' skills or education. Of these, about 60 percent were not assessed economically under the point system. They were allowed in under the "family reunification" category or as "refugee claimants." That number includes more than 210,000 elderly relatives.

The result has been predictable. Despite the highest immigration rates in the developed world, Canada now faces a dire skills shortage. The Canadian Federation of Independent Business said the existing shortage among their membership of smaller businesses is already 300,000. At the same time, the newest arrivals struggle economically. Their poverty rate is dramatically higher than the general population's and is worsening. This has translated into an enormous, uncalled-for burden on taxpayers and on our social services, most dramatically putting financial pressure on the health care system.

The terrorist attack on September 11, 2001, was also another wake-up call, to Canadians as well as Americans, regarding the dangers of lax immigration, visa, and refugee procedures. Unfortunately, the first wake-up call for Canadians should have been in 1999—but was not heeded—when Ahmed Ressam, a member of one of Osama bin Laden's al-Qaeda cells, was caught before he could blow up the Los Angeles International Airport that New Year's Eve. At his trial, it became embarrassingly evident that he and his fellow Algerian terrorists took full advantage of Canada's feckless and loose immigration and refugee system. They were never hotly pursued for deportation, and lived on welfare, while they planned an attack that might have been as devastating as September 11. They also were planning to murder Canadians along the way.

Even after details emerged, nothing changed. In fact, Canadian authorities did not even make it a priority to round up Mr. Ressam's dangerous colleagues, also terrorists posing as refugees. Even after September 11, in December 2001, a new *Immigration Act* was passed, which will actually allow more unscreened persons into the country than ever before and do nothing to enhance the ability to deport undesirables. As things now stand, Canada will continue to be run like a corporation whose human resources department has been put in charge, recruiting too many inappropriate or even dangerous people who can never be fired and who forever will be able to make full use of health care and other benefits.

There is no political party to blame. Both the Progressive Conservatives and the Liberals have mismanaged matters. Many of Ottawa's bureaucrats have been as concerned as I have been about what has been happening. For that reason, over the years many have leaked documents or studies to me. Others have given me leads or anonymous tip-offs. Still others, retired from the government, are joined in a cause to return immigration policy to what it has always been—an important economic lever that has been able to help increase the living standards of Canadians and newcomers alike. Good immigration has been good for the country. Inappropriate or excessive immigration is not. Doing our fair share of humanitarian refugee admissions has been a laudable policy by Ottawa. But a refugee adjudication system has been created that is clearly out of control and not in the national interest. *Immigration: The Economic Case* is an attempt to increase public awareness of this slow-motion national tragedy.

The Debate

Before reading this book, it's important for readers to first consider the issues involved in formulating immigration policies. What needs to be addressed, on an ongoing basis, are the four fundamental questions that underlie any national immigration agenda: How many people should be let in every year in order to benefit the country? Exactly who should be allowed in? How many should be let in for humanitarian reasons? How successful and efficient are government personnel and processes in meeting immigration objectives?

How Many?

Canadian immigration policy since the late 1980s consists of an official immigration target of 250,000 persons a year. This is a departure from the past when numbers fluctuated based on a variety of factors, economic and otherwise. This number is high relative to other developed countries, including the most popular immigration destination, the United States. Canada's target represents three-quarters of one percent of the current population. America's target of 700,000 per year (reality is one million arrive legally and illegally) represents one-quarter of one percent.

Economic arguments in favor of large-scale immigration include a belief that population growth always enhances economic growth; that Canada should dramatically increase its population to become more important, both economically and geopolitically; that immigration is always beneficial because immigrants are entrepreneurial and work harder than native-borns; that lots of immigrants do all the menial jobs native-borns won't do; or that immigration will overcome the negative demographic effects of Canada's aging population with its pressure on government services such as health care and pensions.

Arguments against are: that Canada does not need to increase its population in order to increase prosperity, because the free trade market area provides opportunities for economic growth beyond our borders; that demographically, immigration is only one aspect of population growth and is less important than birth rates, death rates, and emigration; and that large-scale immigration is a costly and foolish notion in a country with relatively high unemployment.

In any debate about immigration numbers, big business favors mass immigration while big labor does not. That is because the one proven economic result of letting in huge numbers of immigrants is that their arrival en masse drives down wages. This benefits employers and consumers through lower wages and, ultimately, prices for goods and services. Unfortunately, such downward pressure on wages harms workers who are forced to compete with immigrants. The result is that their wages and living standards deteriorate.

This means that if Canadians were to decide that the national interest was served by benefiting employers and consumers at the expense of some workers, then policy should ensure that the floodgates remain open. If, on the other hand, the national interest is best served by policies that benefit labor, then having large numbers of entrants is clearly not desirable. Conversely, severe restrictions on numbers allowed into the country would cause economic harm by driving up wages and eventually the cost of goods and services to everyone. The middle ground would be to ensure that the number of entrants is not large enough to harm native-born workers or so miniscule that wages escalate, hurting consumers. This middle ground is where immigration was before 1986—mostly recruitment designed to strategically supplement the labor force—not disrupt it.

Of course, when weighing economic pluses, one must also weigh negatives. What's changed about modern-era immigration is that Canada is now a welfare state. This means that benefits from immigration must be measured against the fiscal costs to governments of providing to immigrants education, health care, legal, housing, infrastructure, welfare and other services. Upon arriving in Canada, a family with one breadwinner, a dependant spouse, and two school-age children would immediately tap the public purse for at least $20,000 per year in health and education benefits alone. (Health care costs are $2,300 per person on average in Canada, and elementary/secondary education costs $5,400 per student annually.)

Policy-wise, that means that if Canadians want only economically beneficial immigration, then admission should be restricted to those persons, or families, with high incomes—and correspondingly high income taxes—who can pay their way. Alternatively, admission could require immigrants to pay for these services out of their own pockets for a period of time. This is what Australia has enacted recently when it comes to health care. Parents, if sponsored by their offspring, must pay for their own medical costs for 10 years. In Canada, the only entitlement that immigrants are denied immediately is old age security. They must first fulfill a 10-year residency requirement. However, they can claim health care immediately and even welfare if their sponsors renege.

The American Commission on Immigration Reform (funded by governments) embarked on a landmark study of such cost-benefits concerning immigration in the American welfare state. In 1997 it concluded that Washington should cut in half its average intake from one million (which includes 100,000 refugees per year) to 500,000 immigrants per year. Figures showed how too many immigrants meant diminishing economic returns. Such a study has never been undertaken in Canada, but if the Commission's conclusion were applied here, that would mean the ideal number of immigrants and refugees Canada should admit should be reduced to only 50,000 per annum.

Who?

Canada's system requires that immigrants must earn sufficient points to be admitted. (Exceptions are sponsored relatives or refugee claimants.) In 2002, the requisite number of points was increased to enhance the calibre of incoming immigrants, said the minister of the day. But this is almost irrelevant because, since 1986, there has been a dramatic shift away from economic to humanitarian immigration in the form of either family reunification or refugee claims.

Arguments in favor of family reunification maintain that this policy is a stabilizing social force that enhances assimilation. Members help one another find housing, jobs, and services. Parents and children are together in a family unit. Child-rearing responsibilities can be shared between generations. Sponsors pledge to look after their relatives' financial needs so there's no cost to the taxpayer.

Those opposed say that open-ended family reunification brings in unqualified people who become dependent upon families and the welfare state. They argue that large-scale immigration has resulted in huge enclaves that impede assimilation and prevent immigrant offspring from succeeding as citizens. Still others point out that the educational level of sponsored relatives is too low for them to be able to cope or compete in a highly technological economy.

Family reunification begs a subset of other questions: How many people should someone be allowed to sponsor? Should immigrants or refugees on welfare be allowed to sponsor relatives, as is now the case in Canada? Should sponsorships continue to be extended beyond spouses and children to parents, grandparents, aunts and uncles, nieces and nephews, adopted children, and significant others? Should family reunification be restricted only to those periods when unemployment in Canada is low? Should sponsors post a bond to ensure that relatives do not become a burden on other taxpayers?

Refugee claimants, or asylum seekers, are a special category of humanitarian immigration, and their arrival has become a political hot potato in most developed countries. This is because of the massive increase in the numbers of claims in Europe and North America in the past 15 years. It's been in the tens of millions.

The issues involving refugee claimants include the following: how many refugees should be admitted in order to fulfill international treaty obligations? What is the proper definition of a refugee? Should refugee claims be entertained only from persons whose countries are guilty of human rights violations? Is Canada letting in *bona fide* refugees, or are most simply queue-jumpers?

According to United Nations figures, Canada is doing more, compared to other developed nations. Between 1990 and 1999, Canada let in an average of 25,000 refugee claimants per year, jumping to 44,000 in 2001. The U.S. has been accepting 100,000 per year, Australia 10,000 per year, and the United Kingdom 37,400 per year. The other three countries have reduced their intake since the late 1980s by tightening procedures and criteria.

Canada's percentage intake of refugees is second only to Denmark's among developed nations, according to the UN. Between 1990 and 1999, Canada's officially acknowledged average rate of acceptance was 52.1 percent,

France's was 20 percent, Germany's 7.6 percent, the U.S.'s 17.9 percent, and Australia's 14.6 percent. Some critics say the unofficial acceptance rate by Ottawa is even higher. Are these real refugees? Are Canada's procedures irresponsible or inept?

The growing number of refugee claims here also raises the issues of terrorism and public safety. In the months following the September 11, 2001 terrorist attack, a raft of antiterrorist legislation was passed by Parliament without any appreciable change when it comes to immigration. In the nine months after September 11, some 26,000 refugee claimants have been granted temporary residency in Canada, many of whom are from countries in the Middle East, such as Afghanistan and Pakistan. Canada's practice of letting everyone in who claims to be a refugee, then asking questions later, is a public policy matter of grave interest to Canadians and Americans too, with whom we share the world's longest undefended border. Are we safe or in danger?

Another issue is the number of fugitives from the law, including Americans convicted of, or sought for, crimes, who have come here and been granted refugee status. Are Canada's refugee procedures appropriate in these cases or not? Or do they expose the public to danger?

How Successful Has Implementation Been?

Assume Canadians agree with current immigration policies. That's all very well and good, but policies, even accepted ones, are only as effective as their execution. Unfortunately, like so much of what Ottawa has delivered in terms of programs over the years, its immigration practices have been questionable. Examples throughout this book abound as to how Canada's system has been defrauded, abused, or ignored. There are many incidents of departmental malfeasance and neglect. There are huge legal problems with deportation. Are these problems out of line? Are there enough people to do the job properly? Are they being properly managed? Or is the federal government doing a good job in difficult circumstances?

Current policies were also supposed to deliver lots of good people to help build the economy. So why is it that despite the most generous immigration target in the world, it can take years for an engineer from the U.S. or the European Union to gain entry to Canada, while the relatives of an immigrant, with or without education or skills, can enter considerably faster? Is this why, despite huge numbers of entrants, skills shortages exist?

A case in point is that Canada faces a physician shortage, yet 5,000 physicians, permitted to immigrate, are cleaning houses or driving cabs because they are denied entry by Canada's protectionist colleges of physicians and surgeons. Even credentials obtained in the U.S. or E.U. are rejected, and in 2001, only 25 internships were made available in Ontario for foreign-trained physicians. The problem with foreign credentials has been so severe, for other medical professionals as well, that in 2002, Ottawa instructed immigration officials to deny entry to anyone with medical training. Why didn't Ottawa ensure that these people had recognized credentials before admitting them? Why doesn't it help fix the problem once they are here? Similar problems exist for engineers and teachers, yet thousands continue to arrive who will find their credentials useless. Why is this?

Another problem is Ottawa's inability to adapt or react quickly to crises. In a quickly changing Global Village this can be costly. When an inaccurate television documentary in the Czech Republic in the early 1990s billed Canada as a safe haven for anyone, thousands of uneducated Gypsies were inappropriately allowed into the country as refugees before barriers were erected. When refugees already relocated in the U.S.—including several thousand from Somalia and hundreds from Tibet—cynically began swapping their U.S. status for Canadian, to get our more generous welfare-state entitlements, they should have been blocked at the border immediately. They weren't.

• • •

Immigration should be the centerpiece of economic policy, but in Canada it's rarely questioned or debated. This is totally inappropriate because whoever is allowed to join Team Canada today will help determine how prosperous our country becomes in the future. That's certainly the lesson from the past, which is why immigration issues must be monitored and re-addressed routinely, especially in a rapidly changing world. To find out what recent immigration has wrought, read on. Then judge current policy for yourself.

The History

The First Waves

Between 1852 and 1896, 1,892,000 people immigrated to Canada, but 2,190,000 left. Some went south of the border to find work in New England's factories and about one-third decided to go home to Europe. The loss of people, mostly to the United States, has been, and remains, a perennial Canadian problem. "Never in the world's history, except in the case of Ireland," wrote O. D. Skelton, Prime Minister Wilfred Laurier's biographer, "had there been such leakage of the brains and brawn of any country."

In 1901, the Canadian government decided to do something about its 19th-century brain drain. That year, it launched an ambitious economic development strategy based, in large measure, on immigration. The problem was that Canada's population of 5,371,000 was not spread out, and only 400,000 persons populated the prairies. Winnipeg native Clifford Sifton was appointed minister of the interior by Prime Minister Wilfred Laurier.

His special mission was to entice farmers to fill Western Canada's empty wheat country. He first convinced the railways to open 22,500,000 choice acres of land they had been granted as an incentive. Then he offered quarter-sections of farmland, or 160 acres, to qualified immigrant farmers through his aggressive advertising campaign in northern Europe and the United States called "The Last Best West." He also hired agents to recruit people.

"They were coming by the tens of thousands. It was called 'the Canadian miracle'," according to Alan Phillips, author of *Into the 20th Century*, published in 1977.

In addition, Mr. Sifton decided to stem the flow southward by recruiting American farmers northward. An extensive advertising campaign was launched there, using newspapers, lectures, and testimonials from ex-pat Americans who had been successful in Canada. The strategy worked, and Americans, mostly from Iowa and Nebraska, headed for the foothills of the Rockies and snapped up thousands of acres of its deep, rich soil. American novelist Oliver Curwood worked for Mr. Sifton for two years on his campaign and noted that Alberta was turning into "a typical American state." The *Toronto World* newspaper ominously called it "The American Invasion" or "The American Peril."

Then the cunning Mr. Sifton used this paranoia to great advantage and launched a patriotic public relations campaign in Britain to recruit farmers from there. "We must not sit back any longer and watch one of the most promising daughter lands being peopled by settlers of alien blood," said an editorial in Britain's *Fortnightly Review*. Immigration from Britain alone soared to 50,000 in 1904 from 10,000 in 1900.

The prairies became Canada's first multinational region. British farmers tended orchards in British Columbia or raised purebred cattle and horses in Southern Alberta. Mormons from Utah settled around Lethbridge. Many different peoples—from Poles to Ukrainians to Hutterites, Germans, Doukhobors, and Dutch—populated the prairies. Mr. Sifton's bold initiative paid off in spades. In a handful of years, by 1910, he was able to grow the prairie population by 2,000,000 by giving away farmland. This mass migration turned Winnipeg into a boomtown, which, by the outset of the First World War, could boast of having the world's largest grain elevators and biggest railway yards. Canada became the fastest-growing country in the world, population-wise. Wheat production soared to 78 million bushels a year in 1911 from 18 million in 1896, making Canada the world's largest exporter of wheat and the Winnipeg Commodities Exchange the world's largest bourse of its kind. "Wheat financed the modern nation and immigrants grew the wheat," wrote historian Alan Phillips. "It was the immigrants, most of them poor, who made the country rich. It was these aliens who gave us a national economy."

Even after the wheat lands were nearly settled, millions more Europeans clamored to escape the looming war and military conscription. In the four years between 1910 and 1913, a tide of 1,394,753 poured into Canada's cities, mostly Winnipeg, Montreal, and Toronto. Naturally, such a massive influx also created social problems. In his *Strangers within Our Gates*, Winnipeg clergyman J. S. Woodsworth lamented the slums, child labor, and impoverishment suffered by thousands of foreigners living in the city's north end, known as the "Foreign Quarter." There was no social safety net in the country except for families and charities, so the churches and others mobilized and helped relieve some of the suffering. The First World War and rapid industrialization in the cities eventually put the new arrivals to work for better wages and benefits.

What is important to note is that while most immigrants were poor, so were most native-borns. Immigrants were also nearly as educated as native-borns and already urbanized. According to Harvard economist George Borjas in his book on North American immigration, *Heaven's Door*, about 87 percent of the newcomers were literate in some language, compared to 96 percent of native-borns. And the European immigrants who did not end up with their own farms were urbanized when most were not and when the industrial revolution was yielding plenty of opportunities. American studies show that the turn-of-the-century immigrants earned only 8 percent less than the average American earned and soon caught up. The situation was more or less the same in Canada. Those who struggled also had the option, in those days, of easily emigrating south to find work.

The Next Waves

Immigration, to both the U.S. and Canada, slowed to a trickle during the Great Depression and Second World War. With rampant unemployment, and misery everywhere, governments could not justify attracting foreign workers. And nobody wanted to immigrate in troubled times because there was no social safety net to stave off starvation if work was nonexistent. In the years leading up to the Second World War, when Europeans desperately sought escape again, countries continued to keep their borders shut, except to a privileged few with good political connections or wealth. In 1942, only 7,576 people arrived in Canada, the lowest number since 1860. In Canada, the Immigration Branch had become, strangely, part of the Department of Mines and Resources. This was probably because immigration was targeted at recruiting miners willing to work in the country's most remote regions.

After the war, Ottawa slowly began opening its doors to various European refugees, huddled in camps and unwilling or unable to return to their countries of origin, many of which had fallen under communist control. Ottawa agreed, beginning in 1947, to allow in 165,000 of these displaced persons for humanitarian reasons. Another 40,000 "war brides," or spouses who married Canadians serving abroad, began arriving after armistice.

The Netherlands, a war ally, also asked Canada to take 30,000 Dutch farm families whose lands had been flooded. They worked mostly on farms in B.C. and Ontario. Likewise, tens of thousands of Poles, also allies, were admitted, most of whom were educated along with equivalent numbers of Baltic refugees allowed in as domestic workers. Similarly, the United Jewish Relief brought in 22,000 refugees and the Unitarian Service Committee of Canada, along with other churches, sponsored many more. In May 1947, as the first refugees from camps began to arrive, the Province of Ontario launched an ambitious immigration drive. The Drew Plan, named after Premier George Drew, was an effort to restock the country with Britons. An advertising campaign and cheap fares enticed 196,000 from the United Kingdom in the latter years of the 1940s.

In 1951, the federal government responded to worker shortages by embarking on another intentional, and sizable, recruitment drive. That year, the country's population was 14,009,400; during the next 30 years, until the 1981 recession, Canada received another 4,949,000 immigrants, overwhelmingly from Europe and the United States. During this period, the brain drain to the United States was sizable, totaling 2,185,000. But at least it was less than half of the number of newcomers who came to Canada.

The Birth of Multiculturalism

Between 1951 and 1961, Canada's immigration drive was restricted to Britain, Ireland, and certain parts of Europe. In the 1960s, Canada, like the United States, began to open up its doors to Third World countries. The Americans abandoned their quota system, based on national origin, amid concerns that it was thinly disguised racism. After 1967, American immigration requirements allowed entry to those who had money, a sponsor, or a job offer, providing it was proven that an American could not fill the position. While those rules were strict, loopholes and lax immigration procedures beginning after the Second World War permitted a flood of migrant Mexican workers and their families into Texas, California, and other border states, legally and illegally. The result has been a different kind of immigration problem for the Americans: By 2000, some 20 million Mexican Americans lived in the United States, equivalent to one-fifth of the population of Mexico itself. Also during this time, immigration authorities allowed several million more people in from U.S. protectorates such as Puerto Rico and the Philippines.

Canada took a different path. It opened up its system to non-Europeans in 1961, but controlled the flow more successfully than did the Americans through the point system. It largely restricted entry to those with jobs, desirable skills, or education. Points were given based on age, education, proficiency in English or French, occupational credentials, and other factors such as health. There were 112 potential points, and applicants who racked up 70 points were admitted. For instance, if they were between 21 years and 40 years of age they would get 10 points on a sliding scale. If more than 49 years of age, they would get zero. If they had a professional or graduate degree they would get 16 points. If they were a dropout, zero. If they had a job and some family they would rack up a handful of points. Knowledge of English or French were also worth points.

"Not surprisingly, this 'filtering' [point system] has a major impact on the skills and economic performance of immigrants in Canada vis à vis their counterparts in the United States," wrote Professor Borjas in *Heaven's Door*. "Immigrants in Canada—relative to Canadian natives—have higher skills and higher wages than immigrants in the United States. In 1980, for example, the newest immigrant arrivals in the United States earned about 28% less than natives and had almost one year less of schooling. In contrast, the newest immigrant arrivals in Canada earned 16% less than natives [initially, before surpassing them], and had one more year of schooling. In short, the Canadian point system 'works' because it generates a more skilled immigrant flow.

"Despite its arbitrariness, the Canadian point system performs a useful function: it selects those immigrants who the Canadian authorities decided were most beneficial for the country," said Professor Borjas. "By restricting the entry of persons who are 'too old' or 'too unskilled' or 'doing the wrong kind of job,' the point system attempts to match immigrant skills with labor market needs and reduces the fiscal burden that immigration would place on Canada's generous system of public assistance."

The point system sought quality immigrants, but establishing the correct quantity was also an important policy goal. Canadian immigration targets were adjusted annually and based on labor market conditions and requirements. The Department of Employment, Manpower and Immigration was created to forecast needs and respond with recruiting drives abroad. Fluctuations were significant. For instance, in 1950, Ottawa allowed in 73,912 persons; in 1951, 194,391; in 1961, only 71,698; and then in 1967 (during the height of the Vietnam war), 222,876.

Both countries also allowed immigrants who had settled to sponsor relatives, a category known as "family reunification." The idea behind this policy was humanitarian, to unite families separated by war, and to help immigrants assimilate more easily by having their closest loved ones with them. Canada's reunification rules were more generous than America's, or those of most other countries, because it allowed in grandparents, parents, and siblings. These relatives were not evaluated under the point system. In return for this privilege, their sponsors agreed to financially support them for 10 years so that they would not be a burden to the rest of society. In practice, there were few sponsorships during the 1960s, 1970s, and 1980s. An average of one sponsored relative came for every nine independent or "economic" immigrants who arrived.

Immigration aggravated the Quebec political situation. Francophone Quebecers urbanized later than most other native-born Canadians and, as young francophones headed for urban areas, they found themselves behind anglophones and immigrants in terms of education, economic opportunities, and earnings potential. This reality fuelled resentment, contributed to unrest, and helped foment the "Quiet Revolution."

Concern about this contributed to the election of Pierre Elliott Trudeau, a bicultural Quebecer who dominated Canadian politics for a generation. As prime minister, he dramatically changed the course of policy. He brought about bilingualism of the civil service (a form of affirmative action program for francophones), dismantled the symbols of British hegemony, and encouraged "multiculturalism," or the recruitment of immigrants from countries other than the British Isles. In the 1970s, British immigrants lost traditional privileges such as easy entry and the ability to vote in Canadian elections immediately upon arrival.

The policy of large-scale immigration, notably to Quebec, was supported by Trudeau and subsequent prime ministers as a means of fostering national unity. The more immigrants living in Quebec, so the argument has been, the less support there will be in that province for secession. The secessionists certainly felt that immigration undermined their project. They required the children of immigrants to attend French-language public schools in the hopes of converting them to their beliefs. But immigrants voted "no" *en masse* in two referendums, and former Quebec Premier Jacques Parizeau blamed his 1996 referendum defeat, by about 50,000 votes, on "ethnics and money." That racist remark forced him to resign, but it revealed his dislike of immigration.

Mr. Trudeau's initiative and push for "multiculturalism" was accompanied by a great deal of hype and hoopla. It became a national religion, and was billed as evidence that Canada was a more tolerant nation than most. The Liberal party, through the promotion of the concept of multiculturalism, seized the opportunity to brand itself as the pro-immigration party to woo immigrant voting blocs. In political terms, multiculturalism became somehow synonymous with tolerance and high immigration levels, and anyone who dared to criticize high immigration levels was labeled as intolerant or an enemy of multiculturalism.

The Latest Wave

A new era in Canadian immigration began in the mid-1980s, when the Mulroney government established two new policy objectives: Firstly, more newcomers were needed to grow the economy faster and, secondly, huge numbers were needed to solve the problem of the demographic aging of the country. The population argument was that mass migration of young people would lower the age of the country to avoid the problem of too many retirees and too few workers. The Conservatives' traditional supporters, the business community, fully endorsed the notion. This is only natural because huge immigration numbers flood labor markets, driving down wages and driving up prices for products and services by increasing demand.

In 1985, the Conservative government instituted sweeping changes. That year, family reunification was given priority. This meant that the grand-parents of an immigrant could get into Canada more quickly than a points-assessed British tool and die maker or a software engineer from New Delhi or Buffalo. Next, in 1986, the Tories decided to attract more well-heeled immigrants by creating two new "business" immigrant categories—the so-called investor and entrepreneur immigrant classifications. These people, and their families, were fast-tracked for entry if they met certain financial criteria. "Entrepreneur" immigrants were required to start and operate a business employing Canadians. "Investor" immigrants were allowed in if they invested in Canada a certain amount of money—generally, at least $250,000.

In 1989, the Mulroney government hoisted the annual immigration target to 250,000 a year for five years. This was a dramatic departure because it meant that employment prospects and immigration targets were no longer linked. The intention to bring 1,250,000 people to Canada within five years was even riskier considering that the economy at the time was in a serious recession with high unemployment rates. Employment and immigration were divided, and a completely autonomous Department of Citizenship and Immigration was created. To make this bold new scheme come about, the empowered immigration department in Ottawa became a growth industry. In 1989, an additional $500 million was allocated over five years to implement the new policy, despite severe budget restraints imposed on all other departments.

This shift to huge immigration levels was also in sync with the ideology of free trade—free trade in goods, in services, and in people—that the Mulroney government had successfully promoted. Some enthusiasts, including Mulroney cabinet ministers, even mused aloud about accepting 750,000 immigrants per year. By contrast, the United States, with a population of 280 million, had increased its official immigration target in the early 1990s to only 700,000 (though in reality, an average of 830,000 came annually during the 1980s and 1990s, and one million in the 1990s).

Canada's announced level meant that, for the next five years, the country would try and assimilate, despite higher unemployment rates and lower economic growth rates than the U.S., four times as many immigrants per capita as the Americans thought they could handle. To put Canada's ambitious goal into perspective, if the Americans had adopted the same immigration goal as Canada's, but in proportion to their population, they would have aimed to import 2.3 million people per year, an unwieldy immigration flood equivalent in size to the population of Greater Montreal. The Conservative's five-year plan of 250,000 immigrants annually was continued by the Liberals, who won federally in 1993.

The Refugee or Asylum-Seeker System

At the same time as immigration targets were boosted, the country lost control of its refugee determination system. By definition, a refugee (also called an asylum-seeker) is a person fleeing persecution. And Canada, to its credit, has a history of helping such persons. The end of the Second World War, and the capture by the Soviet Union of the Baltic and Central European nations, resulted in the displacement of millions of Europeans. Most found homes in neighboring countries, but one million refugees were in camps at war's end.

In 1948, the newly created United Nations established the High Commission for Refugees. By 1951, this Commission forged the "Convention Relating to the Status of Refugees." Canada chaired the committee that drafted the Convention, but did not sign it for another 18 years.

The UN Convention defined a refugee as a person who, as a result of events occurring before January 1, 1951, found himself or herself outside his or her country because of a well-founded fear of persecution for reasons of race, religion, nationality, membership in a particular social group, or political opinion. In 1951, the Convention applied only to Europeans. But in 1967, a protocol was attached, which included refugees from anywhere in the world without a time limitation. Two years later, the Trudeau government finally signed the Convention.

Despite its delay in signing, Canada did its share. After the communists invaded Hungary in 1956, Canada accepted 37,000 Hungarian refugees. In 1968, it accepted 12,000 Czechs, who fled after a similar invasion. In the early 1970s, Canada took in 7,000 Ugandan Asians who had to leave their country by order from its dictator, Idi Amin. Thousands more Chileans came here following the Pinochet coup, and 100,000 Indochinese came as a result of wars there.

"In 1986, the United Nations High Commissioner for Refugees awarded Canada the Nansen Medal for outstanding service to refugees," wrote William Bauer in a newspaper article. Bauer is a former member of the Immigration and Refugee Board and now an outspoken critic of Canadian immigration and refugee policy. "For the first time, the medal was presented to an entire people because the achievement belonged to governments, groups and individuals throughout the country. For many Canadians, the medal was proof that we had finally recognized our responsibilities to refugees and could stop feeling guilty about our misdeeds in the earlier part of the century [failing to help European Jews flee Hitler]. This sense of guilt, however, lingers; it is part of the reason Canadians are easily discouraged from any frank or sustained discussion on immigration or refugee policy."

The Convention stipulated that signator countries had to provide refuge to those who were determined to be refugees according to the criteria it set out. By the end of the 1980s, when the Soviet Union began falling apart, Eastern Europeans poured into Europe claiming refugee status. Likewise, people from Third World countries began arriving in large numbers in Europe, the United States, Australia, Canada, and New Zealand claiming to be refugees. An industry of lawyers, consultants, and people traffickers sprang up globally. Eventually, Canada became a refuge of choice for a number of reasons. Firstly, it was a back door entry to the United States. Secondly, the country had become, by 1985, one of the easiest in the world to get into, even for fugitives from the law. The first group to illustrate this unfortunate reality comprised 300 Iranians who came in 1983 to Montreal asking for refugee asylum. Five years later, about 100 were convicted of heroin trafficking and violent crimes. They were all gang members.

"None were deported," wrote Charles Campbell, retired vice chairman of the Immigration Board in his book, *Betrayal and Deceit*. "Since Canada opposes capital punishment, deportation to countries where severe punishment is part of the legal process is not even considered an option. Thus, an invitation is extended to the criminals of the world to take advantage of our generosity and in the process the destruction of Canadian lives is tolerated by the Canadian government."

Claims by others began to flood the system as word spread among traffickers in people that Canada was so easy to enter. These smugglers—called "coyotes" in Latin America, "snakeheads" in Asia, and "shleppers" in Europe—charged as much as $50,000 per person, depending upon the degree of difficulty involved. Canada's refugee acceptance rate was four times higher than Europe's or America's, and the word went out.

For instance, Sri Lankan refugee claimants in Canada set up consultancy businesses to help others get in as "refugees." Upfront fees were collected, and printed instructions were sold as to what to say and what not to say. This systematic exploitation of Canada's refugee and immigration systems led to some spectacularly successful results. In 1994, Canada accepted 99 percent of Sri Lankan applicants (from the Tamil religious minority), while in the same year the United Kingdom only accepted nine percent. In 2000, Canada accepted 2,915 Tamil asylum-seekers even after the British refugee officials accepted none because they realized what Canadians did not: That under the UN's Refugee Convention, receiving countries could refuse to accept a claimant if they were able to move to another part of their country safe from persecution. This was known as the principle of "internal flight." This principle, if applied, would have blocked the arrival of tens of thousands of young Tamil men into Canada as "refugees"—because they have always been safe in their portion of Sri Lanka. But the inept application of Convention rules opened the floodgates.

"Canada saw the first dramatic sign of this quantitative shift in refugee claims in 1985, when more than a thousand Portuguese arrived, claiming they were persecuted in Portugal because they were Jehovah's Witnesses," said Mr. Bauer. "The claims were bogus, put forward by crooked immigration lawyers and consultants, but they created chaos in the refugee determination system. Shortly after, hundreds of Turks put forward spurious claims to refugee status. The government of the day appeared paralyzed, and, in the end, most of the fraudulent claimants managed to obtain landed immigrant status."

The flood became worse following a disastrous decision by the Supreme Court of Canada in 1985. Known as the *Singh* decision, the court determined that the Canadian *Charter of Rights and Freedoms*, which guarantees legal protections to Canadians, protected anyone who set foot on

Canadian soil. This meant that any refugee claimant could no longer be rejected by an Immigration officer at the border and sent away because he or she had no documents, or had false ones, or appeared to be lying. He or she was entitled to a full-fledged oral hearing inside Canada. This was a disaster because it meant that anyone claiming refugee status at any of Canada's ports of entry was able to enter and enjoy all the entitlements such as a work permit, health care, housing, legal aid, or welfare until a hearing was heard into their case. Numbers ballooned, and the bureaucracy was unable to keep up. Refugee claims leaped from 500 in 1977 to an annual rate of 18,000 by 1990. The system became so overwhelmed that by 1990 there was a backlog of 100,000 refugee claims yet to be heard.

The Liberals, who brought in the *Charter* back in 1982, had been warned about the possibility that it could be used to protect aliens inside our borders. Jack Manion, former associate clerk of the Privy Council and former secretary of the Treasury Board, who also spent 26 years in Immigration Canada, the last three as deputy minister, told a Senate hearing into a new *Immigration Act* in fall 2001 that he warned Jean Chrétien, then justice minister and minister for constitutional negotiations, about the *Charter* extending protection to illegals in Canada.

"I was assured by then Deputy Minister of Justice Roger Tassi that the *Charter* [protection] did not extend to those without legal residency rights. Then came the *Singh* case," Mr. Manion told the Senate committee. "That judgment was a disaster."

Immigration lawyer Richard Kurland said *Singh*—which guaranteed *Charter* protection to aliens here—could have been avoided. He blames civil servants, near retirement, for not listening to concerns from Justice Department lawyers who said that Immigration officers could not merely put claimants on a plane or back in the U.S. without explanation—that as long as they issued reasons, verbally or in writing, the Supreme Court would not require an in-country, full-blown oral hearing for claimants. The associate justices were divided 3–3, and a tie breaker by the chief justice ruled the day.

"If claimants were given reasons and then were put on a plane, that would have made a difference to the court," said Mr. Kurland. "The claimants' lawyers could at least take the reasons for rejection to a court to scream about the decision. The judge would be able to look at the reasons and would say to the lawyer, here's the information and the sources they have and if you're saying they are wrong then prove it. In other words, the burden of proof would have been on the claimant and that would have made all the difference in the world. The bureaucrats were told to tinker with the system to fix it. They didn't and that's why some of them are so mad. The court was simply saying that you cannot give a bureaucrat total control over decision-making without any inspection."

The backlog grew worse. The Mulroney government hired lawyers on contract to rush through approvals to clean it up. At the same time, the government created a revolutionary refugee determination system, which made matters worse. The newly constituted Immigration and Refugee Board (IRB) would adjudicate refugee claims as well as deportation cases involving landed immigrants. Some 180 hearing adjudicators, all lay people called "board members" and not judges, were appointed by the prime minister and drawn from the community at large. They were, in other words, patronage positions. The pay was $87,000 a year plus expenses, and appointments were intended to last around two years.

Hearings were to be held *in camera*, beyond the scrutiny of the press or the public, for the protection of claimants. Every outcome was appealable to the Federal Court of Canada. Each case would be heard by two member adjudicators, and decisions would be arrived at unlike any other "court" of law: an applicant's claim would be accepted if at least one of the two members agreed to let the person into Canada.

Negative decisions were always appealed because claimants had the use of legal aid lawyers. This meant that the board members, both amateurs, had to put their reasons in writing for the appeal court, a skill that usually took lawyers years to master. Many appeals courts overturned board decisions, one might guess, because the writing skills, or legal knowledge, of board members was so substandard. Because board members were judged in terms of the number of decisions that were not overturned, there was more incentive for them to approve claims rather than reject them and invite an appeal.

The hearings were conducted without any of the normal rules of evidence. No witnesses could be called. No cross-examination of the claimant could be conducted by government lawyers, investigators, or members. The claimant's statements were assumed to be true, no matter how far-fetched. One Nigerian claimant said he did not know how he got to Canada because a witch doctor made him disappear and sent him here. His claim was accepted.

"There has been absolutely no public interest served by the refugee system in Canada," said Elizabeth Dodd, a lawyer and refugee hearing officer, who retired from the IRB in 1997. "The system is ridiculous. There is no cross-examination of refugee claimants. It's in the act but it's not done, and there's the absolute inadequacy of political appointees as board members. The Liberals [after their election in 1993] kicked out the Tory appointees, who were well-trained, so they could put in their envelope stuffers and widows. Some can't even write English. One Filipino board member said yes to everyone. Never denied a single claim. Some refugees traveled around the country to get the members they wanted. The problem with having amateurs in these positions is that all negative decisions are challenged, so mistakes are made when writing negative decisions. Some of them couldn't even write a decent sentence, and we used to have to do it [write decisions] for them."

The result of having amateurs involved, and legal aid paying, has been a flood of appeals, continuing backlogs, and an increasing burden on the legal aid system in Toronto, Montreal, and Vancouver (where 90 percent of refugee claimants settle). By 1999, some 58 percent of all the cases before the trial division of the Federal Court involved refugee appeals alone.

At the same time as Canada's refugee determination system was becoming even more powerless to stem the flow of claimants, other countries were tightening their systems. This made Canada's problem all the worse, as the people-smugglers diverted their traffic into Canada. By 1998, an internal Immigration Canada study concluded, "As many as 16,000 illegal immigrants are entering Canada each year with the help of smugglers, costing taxpayers hundreds of millions of dollars. Experts consider most people who arrive in Canada without proper documentation to be linked to smugglers .... The trafficking of illegal immigrants has become big business, police say. Syndicates operate in Canada, the United States, Iran, India, China, Sri Lanka, Pakistan, Hong Kong, Thailand, Nigeria and Brazil. They charge clients up to $50,000 .... Police report that some illegals become involved in drug trafficking, prostitution or theft once in Canada in order to pay their smugglers."

More bad court decisions made the situation worse, as even more *Charter* consideration was extended to refugee claimants. In 1998, the Supreme Court of Canada agreed that a convicted criminal, ordered deported, could apply to remain as a refugee even though he was not facing persecution at home. The case involved a Tamil from Sri Lanka named Veluppillai Pushpanathan. He had obtained permanent residence in Canada in 1985. Shortly after, he was convicted of drug trafficking after his gang of Tamils was found in possession of $10 million worth of heroin. He served his sentence and was ordered deported. In 1991, he was paroled from jail and immediately claimed refugee status. The Refugee Board denied his claim, but over the next seven years he appealed to the Supreme Court of Canada and eventually won.

That decision upset former immigration chief William Bauer, who told an audience of police investigators in 1998: "The 1951 [UN] Convention provides that its provisions do not apply to anyone who 'has been found guilty of acts contrary to the purposes and principles of the United Nations. The Refugee Board decided, under this provision, that the claimant was not a refugee. Naturally, the decision was appealed and two levels of the Federal Court agreed with the decision and dismissed the appeals. The claimant's lawyer then took the case to the Supreme Court, which by a major decision in October 1998, ruled that the Board could not exclude the claimant from a hearing because, in effect, trafficking in $10 million worth of heroin is NOT contrary to the purposes and principles of the United Nations. According to the Supreme Court, only acts which violate human rights fall into this category."

The decision, and failure by the Liberals to overturn it through legislation, rendered Canada's refugee claims process an invitation to fugitives. Besides such court decisions, and political inaction, the members of the Refugee Board and Immigration Canada functionaries made decisions that have strayed from the intent and specifics of the United Nation's Convention on Refugees. For instance, the Convention states that claimants can also be denied sanctuary if they have already received protection from another country or are entering from another "safe" third country that could also take them in. But in the 1990s, border officials began accepting thousands of claimants entering at U.S. border points. And Refugee Board members even began allowing American citizens to land and make claims as refugees, even though they were not under the definition because they came here to avoid jail time, tougher drug laws, or abusive husbands. By 2001, some 100 American citizens or legal residents had been allowed to make claims in Canada. Most were simply stalling extradition procedures. Under the Convention, they were not refugees and, even if they were, could have been sent immediately back to the "safe third country" they came from, or the United States.

Canada's Refugee Board members and judges also began to tamper with the definition of "persecution," contrary to the intention in the United Nations' Convention on Refugees.

"Persecution is not defined in the *Immigration Act*," said Mr. Bauer. "The Canadian courts have held that there should be an element of persistence, repetition or systematic infliction of harm. A risk of random and arbitrary violence for a reason unrelated to the definition [of persecution] is not persecution. Discriminatory treatment because of race or religion is not persecution unless it prevents a person from obtaining a basic education or earning a living. Originally, the intention was that the persecution should be meted out by the state or agents of the state."

The definition has been expanded by Canadian courts. Now, a person can testify that he or she was systematically beaten by a spouse and that the government did not protect the victim. This has been enough to gain refugee status in Canada.

The drift in the definition of refugee in Canada prompted 100 participants in the 2001 Francophonie Games, held in Hull Quebec, to claim refugee status immediately after arriving. Here were pampered athletes, the pride of their nations, asking for protection from persecution. The acceptance rate of refugee claimants in Canada is four times higher than in Europe and nearly triple that in the United States. (Europe's rate is 10 percent and the U.S.'s 17.9 percent). Canada officially admits to an acceptance rate of 45 percent to 60 percent, depending upon the year or spokesperson (the UN said Canada's average was 52.1 percent in the 1990s), but this is vastly understated. Through appeals and other maneuvers, few are ever deported, including terrorists and convicted heroin dealers. Not surprisingly, the flood has continued, and the number of refugee claimants who entered in 2001 was a staggering 47,000, or the size of a small city.

At the same time as volumes swelled during the 1990s, the Liberals imposed two severe budget cuts on the Department of Immigration, in 1993 and 1998. The number of Immigration officers, for instance, was slashed to 4,000 from 7,000. The downsizings led to shortcuts. People who claimed refugee status at the border were to be interviewed by a senior Immigration officer and, unless there were serious concerns, would be routinely referred to the Refugee Division. Beginning in 1999, numbers were so high, and staffing so reduced, that the Refugee Division skipped the interview—to save the expense of interpreters at border points. It sped up processing by handing out "refugee kits" to arrivals claiming refugee status, even to those without *bona fide* identity documents. Claimants were automatically allowed into our country, asked to fill out a questionnaire about their background, and were requested to mail it back to the government within 30 days. They were urged to see a doctor. The kit contained information on housing, welfare, jobs, lawyers, and health care.

In other countries, such as Germany, anyone without documentation is refused entry and automatically sent back, at the airline or carrier's, expense. In the U.S., such persons are detained until their veracity and identity can be determined. If their identity is not established within a few weeks, they are deported. Australia decided to build refugee camps for detention until screening could be completed. But in Canada, anyone without identification has been, and is being, set free and asked to voluntarily return for a hearing. Not surprisingly, 20 percent never showed up for that first hearing, nor did they contact the government.

Then there were legal difficulties involved in removals. On January 11, 2002, the Supreme Court of Canada heard two cases involving two suspected terrorists who had been ordered deported years before. Their lawyers argued that they would be tortured if sent home and that they should be allowed to stay because the *Charter of Rights and Freedoms* guaranteed their personal security. The case involved Manickavasagam Suresh (fundraiser and suspected member of the violent secessionist group the Tamil Tigers) and Mansour Ahani, suspected Iranian assassin and secret agent. The Supreme Court ruled that Mr. Ahani could be deported, but it ruled that Mr. Suresh was entitled to another hearing by the Refugee Board where he would be given a chance to provide evidence that he would be tortured back home. In other words, Mr. Suresh could start the whole refugee determination process all over again.

The system is mired in red tape. The Immigration and Refugee Board can order a landed immigrant, a landed refugee, or a refugee claimant deported. But there are a host of appeals possible. With refugees, there is the refugee determination decision, which can be appealed to an internal appellate division. Then it can be appealed to the Federal Court. If upheld, there is the post-determination risk assessment, which can also be appealed. Then there is a pre-removal risk assessment of any deportation order, also subject to judicial review. Finally, claimants can appeal directly to the immigration minister for humanitarian and compassionate consideration on grounds of risk and, if unsuccessful, can also appeal that to the Supreme Court. Even after final disposition of a deportation, the person is let free and asked to deport themselves, unless already in custody, within 30 days. There is no follow-up.

Such an open-ended, permanent refugee-granting system has led to the inevitable. Between 1986 and 2000, a total of 472,857 refugee claimants were granted permission to stay, either as a result of adjudication or by virtue of amnesty granted by various immigration ministers in order to mop up huge backlogs. This was two and one-half times more refugees than Canada accepted following the devastation of the Second World War, and probably more than in all of its history. Naturally, such permissiveness just encouraged more of the same. And in early 2002, a backlog had built up again to more than 90,000 claims, and there was talk of "triaging" or hurriedly rubberstamping approvals.

Immigration Problems

The refugee system was inundated in the late 1980s, but so was regular immigration. In 1986, the federal government instructed the immigration department to make family reunification a priority. Canada, which already had one of the world's most generous refugee policies, now allowed new immigrants and refugees, even those as young as 19 years of age, to immediately sponsor grandparents, parents, and siblings as long, as they could pledge financial support and "prove" earning power. Theoretically, a single immigrant could bring in dozens of relatives. Many did.

The most recent immigrants, mainly from India, Pakistan, Sri Lanka, and China, took the greatest advantage of "family reunification" immigration. For instance, during the immigration that took place between 1951 and 1986, the vast majority of immigrants were "economic," and only a small percentage of entrants were sponsored relatives. Only one in nine immigrants sponsored someone.

But in the 15-year period from 1986 to 2000, Canada admitted a total of 3,035,615 persons, and about 44 percent were family-sponsored; 15.7 percent were refugee claimants; and 1.9 percent were live-in help or retirees. In other words, only 40 percent were "economic" immigrants who had earned the requisite points for entry because they were skilled workers, highly educated, investors, entrepreneurs, or self-employed persons. Nearly one in five of these 3,035,615 have a university or post-secondary certificate, but there are twice as many adults with less than a grade 9 education as exist among native-borns.

In the 30 years after the Second World War, 4,949,000 immigrants had been investigated and approved from Europe and the United States. By comparison, in the 10 years from 1991 to 2000, 2,213,579 immigrants arrived. That represented an average of 221,357 per year compared to the average annual migration level of 165,000 per year from 1951 to 1981.

By the end of the 1990s, applications abroad averaged 300,000 per year, while the number of officers handling the paperwork, enforcement, and entry points within Canada had been slashed in 1993 and 1998 from 7,000 immigration officers to only 4,000. The number of Canadian visa officers posted abroad was reduced to 200 from 300 and, to save money and handle the workload, 900 more locals were hired in addition to the 200 already employed. This was a dangerous strategy because locals were more vulnerable to bribes, nepotism, or threats. In the 1990s, there were scandals involving embezzlement, stolen documents, and fraud in

Canadian overseas missions in Ukraine, Syria, Hong Kong, and Guyana, among others.

Screening is a sham. By 2001, there were only 32 RCMP officers deployed at 20 of the 81 embassy or consulate entry points to look after security and to help undertake criminal and background checks on applicants. At home and abroad, security for computers, databases, and documents such as passport pages or official forms was nonexistent or minimal. In the mid-1990s, one RCMP officer based in Hong Kong made an accusation that the improper passport security procedures in Canada's Hong Kong offices had led to hundreds of members of triads (the Chinese Mafia) entering Canada as landed immigrants.

Malfeasance within the department has been unacceptably high, according to an internal report I obtained. In just one year, between October 1998 and September 1999, there were 34 departmental investigations involving 36 immigration staff members in Canada and another 85 cases involving 83 immigration workers abroad, for a total of 119 cases involving 127 people. According to the report, allegations were serious enough to involve the police in 67 cases, with the rest handled by the department itself. The result was that, at that point, charges had been laid against two individuals; there were ongoing police investigations against 24 more; and 27 people were disciplined following administrative investigations, with 14 fired, seven resigning, three suspended, and three given letters of reprimand. Another 16 cases were ongoing. Allegations ranged from conflicts of interest to preferential treatment; accepting bribes; theft of money, visas, or documents; fraud; harassment; assault; irregular procedures; soliciting sex to process an application; soliciting bribes; obstruction of justice; aiding and abetting; security risks; breach of trust; impersonation; influence peddling; and counterfeiting visas.

After revelations about malfeasance were published in newspapers in March 2000, Citizenship and Immigration Canada issued a document called *Media Lines* for use by immigration spokespersons when handling questions from the press. I obtained copies of those too. "The annual report on malfeasance details the very small number of cases where allegations of malfeasance were founded. On an annual basis the number of founded cases is less than 1.5 percent," it read.

This admitted rate of malfeasance is totally unacceptable, said Vancouver-based immigration gadfly, activist, and lawyer Richard Kurland, who publishes LEXBASE, The International Information Network for Canadian Immigration Practitioners. He also advises other lawyers and monitors such matters as abuses and policies, advises some politicians, feeds information to the press, and lobbies the government for changes.

"The malfeasance counter-spin from the internal communications group in CIC [Citizenship and Immigration Canada] is that only 1.5 percent of employees are bad apples. But if 1.5 percent of all Royal Bank employees were bad apples, the shareholders would certainly have reason to be concerned. Would we accept that 1.5 percent of school bus drivers could drive while drunk? I mean, what the government is admitting is that 1.5 percent of its employees are corrupt or thieves or taking bribes or have other illegal problems. That's the standard they find acceptable. Well, it isn't. Malfeasance is the biggest issue when it comes to immigration. At any given time, the RCMP has five ongoing investigations on the refugee side, involving staff overseas. They have about 25 investigations a year all the time, and they do the investigations themselves and don't bring in outsiders [or police] who are truly independent. This is really unacceptable," said Mr. Kurland in an interview.

In his testimony before the Senate into the new *Immigration Act* in October 2001, Mr. Kurland pointed out the trend. "The monthly malfeasance reports from Immigration Canada show an alarming consistent trend of bad things happening at our overseas missions, directly attributable to these locally engaged people. There have been RCMP investigations and criminal convictions. We are talking about losses of cash in the millions of dollars, bribery, missing visas, and a parade of horrible events."

One case involved 1,000 missing visas. Two others involved theft totaling at least $500,000 in Damascus and another $500,000 theft at the Los Angeles consulate. Other cases involved missing or stolen "port stamps," which allow users to represent themselves as having entered the country when they didn't, in order to establish residency for citizenship purpose. Even more worrisome were the "security risks" contained in the internal malfeasance report. The 1998 report cited seven "possible security risk" cases reported. One was unfounded, one investigation was dropped after the employee resigned, and five were still active. "It would be really helpful for terrorists to know about this kind of thing wouldn't it?" said Mr. Kurland.

William Lenton, assistant commissioner, Royal Canadian Mounted Police, testified at the fall 2001 Senate hearings about such concerns. "In regard to resource allocation, currently we have 32 liaison officers stationed at approximately 20 locations around the world. As you have indicated, they are spread pretty thinly. In many countries there is no representation. We can only visit such countries periodically. We compensate for that by developing working relationships with the police forces in those jurisdictions, where possible, and when they have mechanisms set up whereby they can conduct inquiries. Of course, it takes time. It takes longer than if we had more people deployed. These relationships must be nurtured. We must work with them, which is difficult when the liaison officer only has occasion to visit once or twice a year."

Canada's border, in other words, was "protected" abroad by roughly 1,300 visa officers (1,100 of whom were not even Canadian citizens) and 32 RCMP officers who had to count on help from local police departments which, to be honest, were usually corrupt. Considering the scale of magnitude of the problem, Canada's commitment to program integrity is, obviously, laughable.

"According to the United Nations, there are between 20 million and 40 million undocumented immigrants throughout the world at present. It is also clear that North America is the destination of choice for these people,"

RCMP Superintendent Ray Lang told the Senate. "The degree of sophistication of technology these days makes it very difficult for us in law enforcement to establish the authenticity of the people who are coming to Canada. This is exacerbated by the fact that many of the jurisdictions from which these people come are either wartorn or do not have the types of systems or records that we have come to expect here in Canada. The significant impact of this on Canadian society is not to be ignored. There is a significant cost involved in processing the people who come to Canada, in integrating them, in removing those who are not permitted to stay, and in conducting investigations and prosecuting where necessary."

In 2001, Auditor General Denis Desautels highlighted in his report that the federal government of Canada was at sea in terms of immigration processing and enforcement activities. "We were disappointed to find many of the same problems [in immigration] that we had encountered back in 1990. It's highly questionable whether the department has the resources and the capacity to meet the annual immigration levels set by government. A weak immigration service is putting Canadians in danger because it isn't weeding out applicants presenting criminal, security, or health risks," he said, adding that since 1994 fewer than 2 percent of high-risk applicants had been turned down and that because of overwork "the department is vulnerable to fraud and abuse."

In a series of interviews I had in 2001 with civil servants in Canada's immigration and refugee system, the public was warned that the new immigration act proposed by the Liberals would make the system far worse than it already was. "What is happening now in CIC [Citizenship and Immigration Canada] is preparation for the total destruction of program integrity—to the everlasting misfortune of Canada," said a letter from a senior officer and a dozen other concerned CIC staff. "While the AG [auditor general's] report correctly identifies the real problem as being unrealistically high targets for immigration and an overwhelmed staff trying to cope with this—unsuccessfully and with huge costs in integrity and health and welfare to communities—the current minister [Caplan] intends to heighten the disaster by radically increasing the num-bers to be brought in," pointed out the letter.

In one interview I mentioned how the auditor general's 2001 report made it absolutely clear, once again, that Canada's overseas Immigration officers lacked the resources to carry out their jobs properly, raising the risk of admitting people who pose a medical or criminal threat to Canadians.

"Employees responsible for processing applications in offices abroad are deeply concerned about the present state of affairs and I share their concerns," Mr. Desautels said. The auditor general's staff interviewed over-seas officers and conducted a survey to document employee concerns. They said there is inadequate medical screening; an inability to manage border and other points of entry, notably airports, to keep out undesirables and fraudsters posing as refugees; insufficient research into criminal or other past behavior; and inadequate training of immigration officers. The auditor general noted that in 1998, $750,000 in processing fees for immigrant and visitor applications went missing, while the number of visas lost or stolen had a market value of about $14 million. The biggest problem was that locals infiltrated Canadian embassies and got huge payoffs for getting people admitted into Canada, either legally or illegally.

"There is clear intent to ignore completely the AG warnings," warned the CIC staff in their letter sent to me. "The public face of this will be that it is simply a pilot project to test whether processing can be done faster in Canada at a giant processing centre. This is patent nonsense. What do Canadians have to pay for this in an environment of huge and sophisticated people-smuggling rings, immense networks of false documentation, the unarguable involvement of organized crime and terrorist networks in placing people in Canada?"

The department was also improperly run, said the auditor general. Each year the department receives about $325 million in fees for processing immi-grant and visitor applications—about 70 percent of which is collected in offices overseas. The department, however, is unable to "reconcile accounts," or to verify that the number of visas issued corresponds to the amount of money collected. "It is easy to get around the controls ... and alter or delete certain daily transactions without leaving an audit trail. Few of the officers responsible for monitoring revenue-related operations in offices abroad ... were aware of this situation," concluded the auditor general.

One of the most serious cases involved the Hong Kong High Commission. The RCMP has been investigating the Canadian mission in Hong Kong on and off since 1992, when allegations were made about bribes, tampering with computer databases, and theft of blank visa forms and stamps. Sources said the computers had been infiltrated by locally engaged staff with links to triads. Investigator Brian McAdam alerted Ottawa that 788 files with sensitive background information on criminals and businesspeople had been removed from the computer and that visas had gone missing. There was concern that hundreds of triad gang members had been allowed into Canada.

Two investigators, one from the Department of External Affairs and the other from the RCMP, flew to Hong Kong to look into the case. Despite being told of files being deleted, finding fake immigration stamps, and discovering that local staff had given themselves unauthorized high-level security clearance to issue visas, neither pursued the matter, and the case was closed. RCMP reactivated the investigation in 1995 and worked with the Canadian spy agency.

Corporal Robert Read of the RCMP's immigration and passport section was put on the case in 1996. He said when he took over the file he found gaping holes in the earlier investigations and became suspicious about the lack of follow-up to leads given to some investigators. Immigration officers were given between $150 and $1,000 in "red packets." Cash in red packets is an old Chinese tradition practiced during the New Year and on special occasions. The unanswered question, according to Mr. McAdam's report on the incident filed to an official in the Department of External Affairs, is: "Why would multi-millionaires constantly invite all newcomers from the Canadian mission's immigration section, as well as locally engaged staff, to the horse races and give them thousands of dollars?"

Suspicions have also been raised about staff who received lavish going-away gifts, including one officer who got a Rolex watch. Another is said to have been given expensive gold coins as a gift to his parents. An Immigration officer who was on assignment in Hong Kong went home with $300,000 that he supposedly won at the races.

Corporal Read was looking into these matters when he was taken off the case, after he made allegations about internal collusion about a cover-up. He filed an obstruction of justice complaint in January, 1998, alleging senior Mounties were trying to cover up the issue, which he said involved 30 immigration officials in Hong Kong. He went public in the press, was suspended with pay, and fought dismissal and discipline for violating an oath of secrecy. In April 2002, the RCMP Adjudication Board found him guilty of self-serving and "outrageous" misconduct that brought shame on the force. He was dismissed.

Citizenship and Immigration Canada said in press releases the matter had been dealt with and "appropriate administrative" action taken against guilty parties as the result of a private investigation done by an outside consultant. Punishment ranged from a verbal warning to dismissal, said a spokesperson. Criminal charges were not recommended by the RCMP even though their probe found that 30 officers at the High Commission accepted gifts and red packets.

Bill C-11: The New Immigration Act, December 2001

The Liberals were smug about their immigration and refugee system, despite publicized problems as well as the embarrassment concerning the arrest and conviction in the U.S. of Montreal-based terrorist Ahmed Ressam. They also ignored warnings by the Canadian Security Intelligence Service every year that 50 other terrorist organizations involving hundreds of individuals had set up shop in Canada from abroad. In fact the Liberals cut back on allocations to both CSIS and the RCMP, whose number of officers had dropped to 12,000 from 16,000 in the 1990s. They also did not listen to public opinion polls and internal Liberal party research that consistently showed a growing opposition to immigration and refugee policies by a large majority of Canadians, both immigrants and native-borns. Instead, the Liberals fiercely, even viciously, defended immigration and refugee determination systems for political reasons. To underscore its commitment, in December 2001, the Liberals approved a new *Immigration Act*, called *Bill C-11*.

A new target of 310,000 immigrants a year, or one percent of the population, was established. The new law increases the number of points needed to enter for those applying as "economic" or independent immigrants. Then it greatly relaxes requirements under the "family reunification" category. The new act also increases the maximum age of a "dependent" child from 19 to 22 years. It also permits sponsorship, for the first time ever, of common-law and same-sex partners. It reduces, from 19 to 18 years, the age at which an immigrant or refugee can sponsor relatives. And it reduces, to three years from 10, the length of time sponsors must pledge to support relatives.

As for refugee claims, Canada's new legislation does not deal with issues such as detention and pre-screening, returns to safe third countries, or getting out from under the *Singh* decision by the Supreme Court of Canada. It merely adds another layer of appeal—to the four already available—in the refugee determination process. A refugee appeal board is inserted as an interim step between the initial hearing and Federal Court. As if to underscore the new permissiveness, the Liberals renamed the Refugee Determination Board the Refugee Protection Board.

The Senate hearings into the new *Immigration Act*, or *Bill C-11*, heard testimony by some of the country's highest ranking former immigration and government officials, who warned of future catastrophes. Senators also heard testimony as to how Australia in 2001 had tackled similar immigration and refugee problems. That country added restrictions on family reunification (grandparents have never been sponsorable there). Unless the majority of an immigrant's sisters or brothers were already permanent residents, Australia would not consider further family sponsorships. As for sponsored parents, Australia required sponsors to cover all health service costs through private-sector insurance for 10 years. It also began detaining all refugee claimants until their true identity, and background, could be thoroughly checked and properly considered. If unacceptable, they were automatically deported.

Meanwhile, Canada's then-minister of immigration, Elinor Caplan, tabled the bill weeks after the September 11 terrorist attacks and immediately billed it as antiterrorist—even though it had been drafted months before and not a word had been changed. She also announced a requirement for tamperproof identification cards for newcomers. She claimed the new bill would prevent a war criminal, terrorist, or serious criminal from ever making a refugee claim, because it allowed detention for 72 hours in suspicious cases while background checks were to be made and an ineligibility ruling could be rendered.

But here is the testimony of Janina Lebon, national vice president, Canada Employment and Immigration Union, which represents immigration workers, who commented on the impracticality of detention:

"We are looking at a two-pronged problem. First, the [lack of] resources to do the 72-hour turnaround, and, second, how we accomplish what we already do regularly. As an example, two weeks ago, the Niagara Falls-Fort Erie areas attempted a pilot project of the 72-hour turnaround. I received phone calls from people saying, 'What are we doing? We have refugees sitting in our waiting room and we have our regular immigration to do.' We tell them to wait. They could actually leave and we would not know they have left. There are no facilities to keep them. If you saw the picture, some of the people slept outside with a blanket because there was no way to process them. Fortunately, their director had just come back from an assignment. His first initiative was what he called the direct-back policy. He sent those people back to Buffalo and told them to return, by appointment, within the 72 hours that we can process.

"The law is not in place, but the minister did attempt to introduce the 72-hour process. This was planned for Pearson Airport. The staff basically said, 'Where? We have a sitting room. We are going to keep all of the refugee claimants, maybe 20 every day. Where do we keep our clients who come in that we have to process?' The department is not thinking ahead. That is a major concern. There are health and safety issues. If you keep a client sitting for 24 hours, they will definitely not be in a good mood. There is a potential for violence, and even the officer will not be in the best of moods because of the pressure that is there."

Here is the Senate testimony of former immigration official Jack Manion:

"My interest in immigration dates back 50 years. It led me to join the immigration service in 1953. I spent the next 26 years of my 37-year career in that department, the last three as deputy minister. I was directly involved in virtually every major immigration policy issue in those 26 years, and indirectly involved over the next 11 years by virtue of my roles in the Treasury Board and Privy Council Office.

"With that background, I must state quite carefully that I find Canada's current immigration situation a shocking and scandalous mess unique in the history of that program. Our inability to control our borders is gravely eroding our sovereignty. All of the remarks I will make illustrate views that I held before September 11. On that day and since, my views have only strengthened. The bill before you will help somewhat to tighten up procedures, assuming that it withstands *Charter* challenges, which I doubt that it will. However, it does not address the source of the problems, which is the

1985 Supreme Court judgment in the *Singh* case that extended *Charter* rights to anyone seeking entry to Canada."

"I was concerned about the potential implications of the *Charter* on immigration when it was being drafted. I was assured by the then-deputy minister of justice that the *Charter* did not extend to those without legal residency rights in Canada. Then came the *Singh* case. That judgment was a disaster.

"In 1987, I was asked, as associate clerk of the Privy Council, to co-ordinate the preparation of emergency refugee legislation. When the resulting bill came before ministers, I was asked if it solved the problem. I said it was the best we and the lawyers could do, but in my judgment it would not survive *Charter* challenges and that the only effective solution was use of the notwithstanding clause or an amendment to the *Constitution*. I am not saying that I believe foreigners should be denied all protections of the *Charter*, but I do believe that Canada as a sovereign country must be in a position to make a summary decision in the case of those who have no legal connection to this country, as virtually every other country in the world does.

"Since that time, I have urged every minister of immigration and the current prime minister to deal with this issue. In 1994, I wrote the Honour-able Sergio Marchi, setting out the facts and issues as I saw them. I pointed out, in particular, first, the direct costs of immigration were two to four times greater than the $950 million he had publicly announced, and, second, that the situation would become progressively worse because Canada no longer had the assurance that it could legally control its borders or implement any immigration policy. Immigrants were increasingly self-selected, and Canada was becoming a haven for the world's opportunists. Mr. Marchi did not reply.

"In 1999, at the time of the Chinese boat arrivals, I wrote the Honour-able Minister Elinor Caplan along the same lines, and again the minister did not reply. Two months later, I wrote the prime minister complaining that his minister was ignoring the problem and possible solutions. I would like to take the liberty to quote from that letter portions which summarize my views perfectly: 'My principal concern about the present immigration situation is that no one seems to realize that there is a critical issue of sovereignty here. To those who plead for an open-door, compassionate response to this latest wave of boat people, I say that certainly we should take as many of the world's genuine refugees as we can, but Canadians, and not criminal gangs and unscrupulous immigration consultants and lawyers, should decide how many that should be. That is not only our sovereign right but our responsibility to all Canadians. Secondly, we also have a responsibility and a right to ensure that those we do admit are, as a minimum, not dangers to Canadian health or security. Finally, we cannot continue to spend the billions of dollars we now spend on this uncontrolled problem and deny our immigration service the resources it needs for, first, measures to bring to Canada genuine refugees and those immigrants able and willing to make a positive contribution to this country, and second, to provide effective enforcement services to identify and deal with those who have no legal right to be in Canada or who are threats to our security and well-being.'

"I said also to the prime minister: 'I am also aware that my implicit criticism of the *Charter* and my suggestion that it be bypassed or amended to deal with this problem will not find favor with those like yourself who are justifiably proud of their role in its creation. However, I am aware that the *Charter* was never intended to destroy our sovereignty in the matter of immigration, and surely if there is anything Canadians are noted for, it is our pragmatism and adaptability to changing circumstances.' I did not get a reply to that letter."

Here is another powerful presentation to the Senate in fall 2001, made by James Bissett, former head of Canada's immigration service and ambassador in the Balkans:

"I will focus primarily on what I think is the major weakness of *Bill C-11*, and that is it does not address where Canada is most vulnerable. It does not address the asylum system we have in effect in Canada. Thousands of people arrive every year claiming to be refugees. Most of them are not refugees. They are economic migrants. Sixty to 70 percent are smuggled by international traffickers. They pay big money to get here; Chinese applicants paying up to $50,000 U.S. apiece to get here.

"It should be clear in everyone's mind that they are not refugees. They are people coming claiming to be refugees. We received 37,000 last year [2000]. These are people who simply walk into the country, for the most part with false documents, because you cannot get on an aircraft without a document. They get the documents, they arrive, they make a refugee claim, and then they are home free. We do not know anything about them. Often we do not know where they have come from or even the flight on which they came to the airport. None of them are screened for security. None of them are screened for health or criminality. They are on the loose. That is a very serious threat in the light of what has happened on September 11.

"The proposed bill does not do anything to address that issue, and that is its major weakness, in my view. It will make it just as easy as ever for these people to arrive, probably much easier. There are certain clauses of the bill that will make it much easier for people to come. It makes it much more difficult to get them out of the country. Part of the reason for that is it is difficult to remove anyone from Canada because of the number of levels of review, the courts, and the lawyers who represent them. It makes it almost impossible to get rid of people we do not want. That is the reality.

"In 1999, 58 percent of the cases dealt with by the trial division of the Federal Court were refugee cases. That must tell you something. On the front page of the [Ottawa] *Citizen* this morning is a face that is familiar to me, Mahmoud Mohammad, a terrorist who threw a hand grenade on an El Al aircraft in Athens airport and then machine-gunned some of the passengers. He was put in jail in Greece. The PLO [Palestinian Liberation Organization] negotiated his release. He went to Spain, assumed a new identity and came to Canada in 1987. We found out he was here. We instituted deportation hearings against him, and he is still here. The matter is still in the courts.

"*Bill C-11* does nothing to address this. Indeed, it adds more levels of review. It adds another appeal review at the IRB, and it adds another pre–risk assessment review. After everything has gone through, Supreme Court and all, the lawyer can go and ask for a pre–risk assessment review, which stops everything, and we are back in the business again. In my view, that is unsatisfactory.

"Canada is not the only country that has problems with asylum seekers. It is an international problem. All the European countries, the United States, and Australia have enacted measures to try to control it and better manage it. We have done none of these things. Unlike Europe, unlike the United States and Australia, we have stood by and allowed all of this to happen, and we are not doing anything about it with this present bill," he said.

The concept proposed by civil servants for the new *Immigration Act* in the 1980s permitted Canada to return anyone coming from the U.S., Europe, or any "safe third country." Officials recognized that without this there would be a flood of opportunistic, self-selected persons.

"If people are coming to Canada from the United States or from Europe, we would not allow them to be refugee claimants. They would have to be sent home. They already had protection in the United States and Europe. Those countries look after refugees better or as well as we do .... Three days before the bill was enacted, the minister announced that the bill would pass, but that the safe third country [part] would not be enacted. Those of us who drafted the bill knew it was doomed, and since that time, over 400,000, close to half a million, asylum-seekers have come into the country.

"Many Canadians may feel that is all right. However, I think September 11 has changed that. We are in a different world, and we must get much tougher—and this bill does nothing to make it tougher. I could give a long list of things that the Europeans do with asylum-seekers, and I will do that just to give you an idea of what can be done. All of the European countries have the 'safe third country' concept. If people come to Europe from a country that was considered safe, meaning it is a signatory of the UN convention and has a good human rights record, then they are not eligible to enter its refugee system and are subject to removal by accelerated processes. Germany has a list of countries that are considered safe. All the European Union countries are safe, North America, Bulgaria, and Romania are safe. The list of countries is long, and people coming to Germany from those countries, because they are democratic, have good human rights records, and follow the rule of law, are not eligible to get into the system and clog it up. They are sent home.

"Frivolous claims' are dealt with expeditiously in Germany and other European countries and deportation swift. So are so-called 'abusive claims' or when people come without documents or with fraudulent documents and do not cooperate. These countries have signed readmission agreements with other countries that state 'You must take back your failed asylum-seekers.' In Germany's case, if a country refuses to take back a citizen, Germany cuts off their aid. Also in most of the European countries—certainly France, Sweden, Switzerland, Germany—if an appeal is made, they accept the appeal but remove the individual, pending the appeal. They only return if successful.

"Social assistance is the next area of concern. Many countries do not allow asylum-seekers to work. In the United States there is no social assistance for asylum-seekers, and they are not allowed to work for six months. When they introduced that law, the percentage of asylum-seekers in the United States dropped by 40 per cent. Why? Because most people are not coming into the United States for protection. They are coming to get into a country because they do not want to line up at the immigration offices. There is a strong correlation between the top 10 countries for immigration and the top countries for asylum-seekers, for example India, Pakistan, Sri Lanka, Hungary, and Iran.

"The bill is totally inadequate, and it should be sent back. All the measures that I have described to you are fully approved by the United Nations

High Commissioner for Refugees. Why does this bill not address [those issues]? Why are we not doing these things? We are idly standing by and letting 45,000 people—and it will be much more than 45,000 in a year or two because, with the Europeans tightening up, the traffickers and the smugglers know where the soft countries are—seek asylum here. We have a reputation as being soft on criminals, on security issues, and on asylum seekers. This bill does nothing to address the reality that we are in a post–September 11 world. I am not suggesting that we do anything to deny fundamental justice. I am just saying, 'Look, we are generous, but we cannot be irresponsible.' It is little wonder that our southern neighbours are worried about what we are doing up here because we are not facing up to the reality that many of these people could turn out to be terrorists. I am not suggesting that the 400,000 applicants are, but you do not need more than five or six or 25, as we found out on September 11. We must be much tougher.

"*Bill C-11* broadened the UN definition of "refugees" when all other countries and the U.S. are trying to narrow the meaning. The new law gives anyone protection who comes here and asks for it. That's enshrined and is a huge mistake because no one can be screened before entering Canada again," Bissett said.

Another concern expressed to senators, stated by former ambassador and immigration official Martin Collacott, was that current immigration levels would eventually turn Canada into an intolerant nation. This could happen as millions more unskilled and undesirable immigrants and refugees flood our economy, living in larger and larger enclaves, disrupting the job market, making huge demands on our social services, and committing crimes or acts of terrorism.

"With respect to [family reunification] immigration, it is doing even more damage in the long term to Canada than our refugee determination system. In my brief, I give details on why the government's claims about the economic and demographic benefits of the current immigration program and the proposed legislation are without foundation. They are in conflict with the results of its own research. One of the areas I believe should be of particularly great concern to us is the impact that current policies may have on seriously undermining the spirit of tolerance and widespread acceptance and, indeed, celebration that most Canadians have of diversity.

"We have nurtured and developed this spirit over the last few decades, and we have set an example to the world in which ethnic conflict has become the norm rather than the exception over the years. I am proud to be part of that example. My wife is an immigrant from Asia, and our two sons reflect the new Canada. However, it is becoming increasingly clear that we are placing these achievements in jeopardy because of ill-considered immigration policies based very much on the part of lobbying by special interest groups and attempts by political parties to get votes in the next election," he said.

The government has not studied whether these new populations are being absorbed or whether they are well equipped to adapt to Canadian society. There is no research as to whether strains and tensions are developing that will result in long-term social damage, he said.

"The despicable acts against members of our Muslim, Sikh, and Hindu communities after September 11 is only the first widespread evidence of a reaction. The United Kingdom, where visible minority communities constitute only half the proportion they do in Canada, has in recent months had a number of serious racial confrontations. I wish to make myself clear on this point. Most of Canada's immigrants will continue to come from developing countries and will be members of visible minority groups. However, we must look much more carefully at how many people we need, how they can be effectively absorbed, and who should be selected. We have still not had a serious and open debate on our immigration policies, and now the need is greater than ever. The current policies are to the detriment of the immigrants themselves. I used to describe our programs as leading to a national disaster in slow motion."

Unintended Consequences

"It's just obvious that you can't have free immigration and a welfare state."
—Milton Friedman

The dramatic deterioration in overall immigrant credentials between 1986 and 2000 has brought with it huge social and economic costs. In essence, Canada may have imported a disadvantaged underclass the size of Atlantic Canada and will continue to do so in every future decade unless the new *Immigration Act* of 2001 is scrapped. Most of the new arrivals to Canada since 1986 are inappropriate for our economic needs and will have difficulty prospering in our highly technological, information-age economy. Previous immigration waves were about matching jobs with people. Now it's just about sheer numbers. Worse yet, previous immigrants had the option of emigrating south if work was unavailable in Canada. Now, unskilled or uneducated persons out of work have nowhere to go. Besides, Canada's generous welfare state removes any incentive to leave or to return home. They can live modestly on government assistance and enjoy educational, medical, and housing benefits for a lifetime.

According to a 1996 internal document I obtained, Ottawa's mandarins and ministers believe that immigrants and refugees more than pull their economic weight in our society:

"Some of the economic benefits of immigration include a larger domestic market of consumers, a stable supply of skilled workers, and inflows of financial and human capital. Immigrants also represent a steady source of new demand for housing and for durable goods. At arrival, immigrants earn less than the average Canadian, but their performance improves rapidly through the initial years after arrival. Skilled workers adapt quickly, exceeding the Canadian average as soon as three to four years after arrival in Canada. Family class and refugees are not selected on the basis of their potential economic performance. Nevertheless, after 10 to 14 years, these categories of immigrants also catch up to or surpass the average level of Canadian employment earnings. While refugees may draw heavily on social assistance initially, over time employment earnings replace social assistance as their main source of income."

The analysis was based on "empirical research" consisting of information gathered from the income tax statements of immigrants and refugees between 1980 and 1994. These show their earnings, if any, as well as the direct payments they received such as welfare, old age security, or employment insurance payments. But the "statistical analysis" has glaring omissions and does not include the "soft" costs that immigrants and dependants ring up such as health care, education, housing, legal aid, jail, immigration administration costs, or grants. In other words, Ottawa based its conclusion that immigrants and refugees are economically beneficial to the country on incomplete data.

Another interesting observation is that some of the government's own facts contained in the report reveal the deterioration in the economic capability of the newest wave of immigrants. Its research showed there was a marked decline in labor market performance after 1990, but attributed this to general conditions. "The deterioration during the 1990s compared to that of the 1980s is not an experience particular to immigrants. Younger Canadian workers, another group of new labor entrants, are also suffering from a similar phenomenon," it stated.

That observation actually revealed how damaging policies have been. Unskilled and uneducated immigrants and refugees were taking jobs away from the most vulnerable Canadians in our population, those young or uneducated native-borns.

Professor Borjas, in his *Issues in the Economics of Immigration*, made this observation: "Almost half of the 10.9 percentage point decline in the relative wage of high school dropouts observed [in the U.S.] between 1980 and 1995 can be attributed to immigration .... [T]he adverse impact of immigration on the well-being of workers at the bottom end of the skill distribution has been substantial."

Other experts in this field, however, agreed that while immigration had a larger effect on wage disparity than anticipated, the growing wage gap was also due to the shift in demand for technology skills.

The government's study also said that 14 percent of immigrants who came to Canada under the family reunification category between 1980 and 1994 had taken welfare at some point during the calendar year of 1995, as had 30 percent of refugees. These rates dramatically exceeded the Canadian average that year of 10 percent. An even worse problem was the duration of assistance. Refugees represented only 15 percent of the people who came during that 15-year period, but they collected 41 percent of all welfare payments forked out, in absolute dollars, to newcomers. The study looked at one year, 1992, and said that about 77 percent of refugees went on welfare that year. By 1995, 61 percent of that group were still on assistance. It added, "A relatively high usage of welfare by the family class can be attributed to parents and grandparents category."

No comment was made about this even though, by definition, family reunification immigrants were supposed to be financially supported by their sponsors for at least ten years. Far from justifying the current policies, the analysis did the opposite.

More Bad News

It should come as no surprise to anyone that the financial damage to the country due to the difference in entrants was entirely predictable. In February 2002, the Canadian Council on Social Development concluded in its report that recent immigrants were having a tough time and probably would in the future. Family poverty rates were double the Canadian average, due to family size as well as immigrants' difficulty in finding and keeping jobs. In 1998, 58 percent of recent immigrants were employed all year, below the rate of 70 percent for other Canadians. That year, 6 percent of recent immigrants were unemployed all year long compared with 2 percent among Canadians. Some 11 percent of recent immigrants were unemployed at some time during the year, while just 6 percent of other Canadians were unemployed during the year. This represented some improvement from a few years before, but the figures were still distressing. In 1995, the proportion of new immigrants on social assistance at some time in the year was 19 percent. By 1998, due to an ebullient economy, that number had fallen to 11 percent, still double the average.

The council's report stated that "The economic recovery in the latter half of the 1990s has narrowed the large gaps that existed between recent immigrants and other Canadians. In 1998, recent immigrants—and particularly immigrant women—secured more weeks of work and at higher hourly wages than they had in 1995, and these gains outpaced those of the rest of the Canadian population. As a result, these higher earnings translated into higher family incomes and reduced rates of poverty. While this is clearly good news, it must be recognized that very large employment and income gaps between the two groups still existed in 1998. The poverty rate among recent immigrants was still 27 percent in 1998—double the rate of other Canadian families. Strong economic and job growth seems to be a potent force for greater equality. However, it remains to be seen if the situation of recent immigrants at the end of the 1990s will return to the norm of the early 1980s, when new immigrants to Canada quickly 'caught up' economically to the rest of the population."

The council cited an analysis of census data between 1981 and 1996 that showed "a progressive trend towards lower rates of labor force participation and lower levels of earnings among immigrants compared to the Canadian-born population .... Research by Citizenship and Immigration Canada and Human Resources Development Canada shows that the relative earnings of recent immigrants fell sharply between the mid-1980s and the mid-1990s, even among immigrants who had a university education. A presentation ... indicated that immigrants traditionally 'caught up' to average Canadian earnings within 10 to 14 years of their arrival in Canada, but this has changed since the mid-1980s, particularly for immigrants from Asia and Africa."

"Even when education levels are the same, racialized [visible minority] groups are under-represented in managerial, professional and high-income occupations, and they are over-represented in low-end occupations and low-paying jobs. Again, this is particularly the case for specific racial groups, notably Blacks and South Asians," said the report.

Was this due to racism, lack of language skills, cultural differences, or immigrants lying about their credentials? Whatever the reasons, the problem has been acute and is getting worse. In April 2000, the council documented the deteriorating performance of recent immigrants in metropolitan areas. Only 19.7 percent of those who arrived before 1986 were living in poverty—lower than the 21.6 percent of Canadians living in poverty. But between 1986 and 1990, the immigrant poverty rate shot up to 35.1 percent. After 1991, 52.1 percent of all immigrants in Canada were impoverished.

The Toronto United Way released a study in March 2002 that showed the widening gap between rich and poor in Toronto, adjusted for inflation. This hardly surprises, given that Toronto is where nearly half of all three million immigrants and refugees ended up in the past 15 years.

"Toronto is spinning into decline, and we need action now," said a United Way spokeswoman. The study found that married couples, sole-support parents, and singles in Toronto have seen an average drop of 14.5 percent in their incomes since 1990. The rest of Canada experienced a decline of only 3.7 percent. Called *A Decade of Decline: Poverty and Income Inequality in Toronto in the 1990s*, the study showed an overall decrease in incomes, growing poverty, and a decline in quality of life in Toronto. Families in the poorest neighborhoods made an average of $6,800 less per year, and the wealthiest families made about $11,400 more than they did 10 years ago. The study concluded that there are 14,310 more children living in poverty than there were five years ago. It stated that poverty rates for newborns to 17 year olds grew from 30.8 percent of the total in 1995 to 32.3 percent by 1999, greatly exceeding the national average of 25 percent. It also said that there were 11,300 more seniors living in poverty in Toronto than there were five years ago, an increase in absolute numbers of 40 percent, which is greater than the city's overall population growth. "That increase [of impoverished seniors and children] is bigger than the city of Gravenhurst," said the spokeswoman. She blamed business for the rise in poverty. But the cause is excessive immigration.

I would also blame immigration in large measure for the widening gap between rich and poor income levels in Canada and the United States in recent years. For instance, Japan and Sweden, which have very limited immigration, have not experienced the same increase in disparities. Also, the admission of two million uneducated, unscreened individuals in so short a period of time has diminished Canada's productivity levels compared to the U.S.'s.

In 1998, a report by the federal government, entitled *Employment Stability and the Adjustment of Immigrants*, documented what it called the "disturbing trend" that immigrants were lagging native-borns in terms of employment, earnings, and the ability to get a replacement job once unemployed. Among its observations were that immigrants who came to Canada after 1980 were more likely to become unemployed and use social assistance the longer they remained here, while immigrants who arrived before 1980 were less likely to become unemployed or to use social assistance the longer they remained in the country.

The beginning of the economic harm, resulting from immigration, was documented in a book published in 1995 by the C. D. Howe Institute, called *Diminishing Returns*. Its research was based on immigration figures gathered mostly during the 1980s and into the early 1990s, which makes it out of date, but nonetheless disturbingly prescient, given the acceleration of the situation.

"The economic returns from immigration are still positive for Canada but, due partially to immigration policy and practices over the past decade, are diminishing," wrote Don DeVoretz, professor of economics at Simon Fraser University, who edited the C. D. Howe book. "The declining economic returns have also been an outgrowth of immigration policy after 1978. Expanding immigration in the early 1990s as central Canada's unemployment rose no doubt exacerbated the unemployment in central Canada," wrote Professor DeVoretz. But "economically unscreened immigrants" have added to the country's welfare burden.

"Immigration policy should evaluate the entire household unit and not just the principal applicant. The attributes of an accompanying spouse should add assessment points to the household's application. Diminishing returns are inevitable from the immigration process whenever the majority of the entrants are not economically assessed," he wrote, adding that Ottawa should require sponsors to post a surety bond, "so that Canadian resident taxpayers will not bear any of the major costs of immigration."

The Howe book also noted that in 1985, 9.8 percent of the sampled female immigrants used unemployment insurance while 13 percent of Canadian-born females did. By 1990, one-third more female immigrants were using the insurance. In 1985, foreign-born females were only half as likely to collect welfare as their Canadian-born female counterparts. After 1985, foreign-born females were more likely to participate in welfare programs. Also, when the later arrivals did receive welfare, they received $1,600 more in benefits than were paid to Canadian-born females on welfare.

This deterioration, along with reduced economic opportunities, had already begun to be obvious from the Howe study in 1995. A chapter written by academic Ather Akbari showed that the average public finance transfer from the immigrants to the treasury was positive but declining. From 1980 to 1984, cohorts or sponsored relatives transferred $10,252 per year (taxes paid over and above their use of government services) to the treasury. Between 1985 and 1990, this had decreased to $6,190. During the 1990s, when 1,341,064 of the total of 2,213,579 immigrants were family reunification and refugee categories (61 percent of the total), it is probable that any surplus had disappeared.

A Citizenship and Immigration Canada report, *Facts and Figures 2000*, revealed more damaging information about the latest immigration wave. Based on 1998, 1999, and 2000 figures, Canada accepted nearly 600,000 individuals, even though 43 percent spoke neither English nor French. One out of five entrants was a child under 14 years of age who arrived in Canada without either official language, thus adding a huge burden to Canadian public schools. Of the adults, nearly one-third told officials that they did not intend to work in Canada.

The inability to speak English or French, combined with the clustering of large numbers of immigrants into enclaves, increases the probability that the earnings of immigrants and their offspring will always lag. For instance, an American study showed that immigrants entering the United States without English in 1980 made 25 percent less at the time of entry and closed the gap in wages by only 10 percent after learning English.

Employment and earnings challenges facing these immigrants and refugees have been compounded because so many were allowed in at a time when the economy was struggling to create enough jobs for native-born young people too. Between 1985 and 2000, the economy of Canada created 2,659,900 full-time jobs, or an average of 177,326 per year, fewer than the average of 204,442 adult immigrants and refugees allowed into the country during each of those years (another 20 percent are dependent children). By the end of the 1990s, the job situation worsened but immigration increased to 221,358 per year. To boot, at least that many native-borns entered the workforce each year at the same time.

However, there is one "benefit" for the economy to large-scale unskilled immigration, said Harvard University economist George Borjas in his book, *Heaven's Door*, on U.S. immigration problems. He estimated that the total benefit to the U.S. economy was roughly US$160 billion, due to the fact that immigration drives down the wages of all unskilled workers. Comparable research in Canada bore out a similar result, finding that workers in 47 major industries in Canada suffered wage compression due to immigration. They also lost jobs to immigrants.

"Even though the average native gains somewhat from immigration in this way, this does not mean that everyone in the country gains. There are distinct groups of winners and losers," wrote Professor Borjas. "The winners are the people who employ or use immigrant services, and achieve their economic goals at lower costs. The losers are the people who compete with immigrant workers and experience a corresponding reduction in their income. In practical terms, post-1965 immigration has shifted income away from less-skilled natives toward highly skilled natives and owners of capital."

"Large-scale immigration is a perverse federal Robin Hood scheme that takes from middle- and lower-class workers and gives to the country's most affluent," wrote Roy Beck, an American labor expert, in his book *The Case against Immigration*. He calls for a moratorium in the United States on unskilled as well as skilled immigrants. For instance, he said the American Engineering Association has been asking Congress for 20 years to cut importation of engineers to give Americans opportunities. Bright foreign students are enticed to U.S. universities, crowding out native-borns, with the promise of a Green Card.

"Wage depression between 1973 and 1988 was most pronounced for Americans with less education: workers with some college saw wages go down 6 percent for women and 11 percent for men; for workers with high school, wages went down 7 percent for women and 17 percent for men and for dropouts wages were down 10 percent for women and 22 percent for men," wrote Mr. Beck.

The most vulnerable native-borns have been hit hardest by immigration. A Harvard University study in 2000 showed a 10.9 percent decrease in the wages of high school dropouts between 1979 and 1995—about half of it attributed to immigration. The experience in Canada is probably worse because dropout rates are just as high and immigration is proportionately larger than that of the United States. It is surprising that, given the damage to workers, trade labor unions in North America have not been fierce critics of immigration in the same way they have opposed free trade agreements. They have backed reforms, but their idea of reform is to force immigrant jobs to be unionized in order to swell their ranks.

The experiences in the U.S. show how much the recent immigration of unskilled workers has nonetheless eroded the gains made by the American middle class. The lion's share of America's Third World immigration is from Mexico, the rest from Latin America and Asia.

"Since mass immigration was curtailed in 1924, an additional 20 to 30 percent of the U.S. population had moved into the middle-class ranks by the 1950s. Between 1960 and 1990 the middle-class portion of the U.S.

population has thinned by 8 to 15 percent. By 1979, 12.1 percent of all full-time workers were paid wages too low to keep a family of four above the poverty line. By 1990, the proportion was half again as high, at 18 percent," wrote Mr. Beck.

As early as 1985, the McDonald Royal Commission warned that "a broad consensus is that high levels of immigration will increase aggregate variables such as labor force, investment and real gross expenditure, but cause real income per capita and real wages to decline."

The report by the Economic Council of Canada in 1991 was not quite so negative, but concluded simply that there was little or no economic gain from immigration at that point. It also pointed out that more gains would come from creating a larger market through free trade in North America. Had the council written its report in 2001, it likely would have seen immigration as a negative to the economy, given that 61 percent of entrants are economically disadvantaged.

Even the Organization for Economic Co-operation and Development (OECD) noted in 1995 that Canada, although its recent economic performance was relatively good, would go into steady economic decline unless there were fundamental and immediate changes in government immigration policies. "Because its [Canada's] population is growing faster than that of other leading nations, Canada has to run faster just to keep its place as an above-average performer," said the OECD.

In other words, Canada's economic pie was growing, but the number of persons entitled to pieces was growing faster still. The result has been predictable. In 1980, the income per capita was US$22,007 in the U.S. and US$19,116 in Canada. By 1998, the gap had widened to US$32,413 and US$25,496 respectively.

Another problem, in both countries, has been the increasing dependency on welfare by Third World immigrants. In the U.S., the deep poverty among some immigrant groups is expected to extend into the second and third generations. In California, the cost of welfare and other social services used by immigrants has raised the annual taxes of typical non-immigrant households by US$1,200 a year. In Canada, there have been no such definitive studies, but, for instance, the rate of welfare use here by sponsored parents and grandparents is close to four times that of the general population. Immigrant and refugee welfare costs for Ontario taxpayers amount to around $150 million a year. Applied nationally, that means a total welfare cost of $300 million annually.

The total burden of the latest wave of immigration is considerably worse in Canada than the U.S. because our rate of immigration is higher and our economy has not grown as quickly, nor has it created jobs as rapidly. Moreover, our refugee system has contributed another 472,857 persons (between 1987 and 2000) about whom little is known, except that some estimate their cost, in government-provided services alone, to be $4 billion a year.

Not surprisingly, the federal government has steadfastly refused to undertake its own comprehensive, national cost-benefit analysis, clinging to the self-prescribed mantra that immigration is a net benefit to the economy. Another problem in Canada is that costs are difficult to determine because they are buried in the operating expenses of thousands of provinces, school boards, and municipalities.

In summary, what's changed since previous immigration waves is the total mismatch between the educational and skill levels of immigrants and the requirements of the country's more sophisticated and technological information-age economy. At the same time, Canada's generous welfare state has robbed many newcomers already here of an incentive to work and has also created a "pull factor" to those living abroad to undertake any means in order to get here. For instance, the Philippines has an average per capita income of US$3,000 per year. Therefore, a Filipino immigrant in Canada who lives on welfare and earns cash under the table by cleaning houses or babysitting is still hugely better off because health care and education are also completely free.

As George F. Kennan, a U.S. elder statesman, pointed out in his 1993 book *Around the Cragged Hill: A Personal and Political Philosophy*, where open immigration is permitted, people will pour into that economy until the levels of overpopulation bring about poverty levels that are equal to poverty levels in their homeland. There's a large incentive to get into our economies, driven in large measure by the entitlements of the welfare state.

In January 2000, at the World Economic Forum in Davos, Switzerland, I interviewed China's second-most powerful leader, Vice-Premier Wu Bangguo, about the "pull factor" and how this encouraged people-smuggling. In 1998, 11.36 percent of all immigrants and refugees entering Canada came from the People's Republic of China. By 1999, this had jumped to 15.33 percent, and in 2000, 16.16 percent—or one out of every six newcomers. Concerns on the part of the Chinese government about smuggling were that its own officials were becoming involved in the illegal trafficking of its people, and that the migrants were indentured and often forced to work in sweatshops, criminal organizations, or prostitution.

"The Chinese and Canadian governments must work together to stop this illegal immigration," said the vice-premier. "The people are enslaved by these snakeheads. Our two governments must also pay attention to cracking down on these snakeheads."

Ottawa's response? Then-minister Caplan took a trip to China a few months later in 1999 to urge Chinese migrants to stay at home. The result? The number of Chinese immigration and refugee claimants has risen.

The Demographic Myth

In March 2002, the latest Canadian census revealed that, between 1996 and 2001, the country's population increased by 4 percent, to 30,007,094 from 28,846,761. This, added to the half-decade result between 1991 and 1996, represented a 9.95 percent population increase, or the lowest 10-year increase in the 20th century. Hand-wringers turned out in droves following the release of the census report and repeated the same old myths: bring in even more immigrants because it's important that Canada be bigger than it already is, it's a big empty country, and more immigrants will reduce the problem of an aging population.

This revealed a complete misunderstanding of 21st-century economics. The we-have-lots-of-room school was rooted in the early 20th-century "Last Best West" drive to give away empty farmland to skilled and unskilled people in order to populate the frigid prairies and create freight for the railway. Canada is no longer a gigantic, horizontal band of farmland along the U.S. border that requires millions more laborers to till its soil as a means of lifting us into the economic big leagues. And Canadians do not need to foster a bigger internal market in order to grow world-class industries and become exporters and world-beaters.

That's 19th-century thinking—the kind of process that Sir Wilfred Laurier bleated about when he said the 20th century would be Canada's if we reached a population of 100 million. Such notions, perhaps valid then, were overtaken by two revolutions and one major policy initiative—the industrial revolution, the technological revolution, and free trade. After 1989, and the launch of the free trade agreements with the United States and with Mexico, Canadian business has had access to the largest, most prosperous marketplace in the world. Since then, exports have tripled.

Population-boosters also failed to realize that large tracts of land don't matter a bit, apart from resource exploration. Canada has become a handful of city-states, led by Toronto, Vancouver, Montreal, and Calgary. That's where virtually all the immigrants go, and that's where most of the in-country migration goes. Wealth creation is about clusters of economic activity facilitated by reasonable taxes, good infrastructure, educated workers, vibrant markets, good distribution networks, and research aptitude. It's about quality, not quantity, of workers.

The point is that size does not matter anymore. In fact, it's a problem. Ask yourself: if a country's population really matters, then why don't India, China, and Indonesia rule the world? Why aren't they the world's richest countries? Canada already has enough people to maintain its lifestyle and, at the same time, create wealth in order to look after an aging population. The brain drain to the U.S. is a problem, but strategic immigration can replace those who leave.

Sweden, for instance, is already demographically as old as Canada will be in 30 years' time and has dealt successfully with the issue without increased immigration. It has done this by maximizing the potential of its existing workforce. This has been accomplished through education, by passing laws to encourage part-time work for parents, by ensuring day care spaces, and by providing incentives for people to postpone retirement or work part-time. More importantly, its industries have expanded aggressively into export markets and invested heavily in automation and technological advances, thus greatly enhancing the productivity of the workforce. Studies show such productivity gains can offset any deleterious effect of an aging, retiring population that is growing faster than the workforce that supports it.

Canada can easily undertake these reforms. And it should. Productivity lags badly already. Besides, we already have a huge underclass that needs bootstrapping first, through education, and that should be done before more people without education are brought into the country. Immigration should be reduced and be made strategic again, and not open-ended as is now the case.

In March 2002, the Institute for Research on Public Policy, a Montreal think-tank, refuted the "immigration will solve the aging population" argument. "While we cannot ignore the challenge it [aging] poses to public expenditures and economic growth, we should not forget that it also generates new opportunities," said the study, called *The Bright Side: A Positive View on the Economics of Aging*, by University of Ottawa economics professor Marcel Merette. He argued that rising wages among a better educated population, and an increase in the number of older workers in the labor force, will help offset increases in costs for health care and old age security. So will the arrival of more taxable income from registered pension plans.

"My expectation is that with the aging of the population they [young people] will come out [of school] to what could be three or even four job offers, like the generation that graduated in the 1950s and 1960s," he told the Canadian Press in 2002.

He projected that by 2046 there will be 10.8 million elderly in Canada, up from 3.7 million in 1997, with accompanying increases in medical costs. A Health Canada study found per-capita health care spending on seniors is more than three times that for the population as a whole, or roughly $8,068 for those 65 years of age and older. But the aging workforce will be better educated and more productive, thus capable of generating the taxes necessary to provide services for all. They will also be encouraged to work later into their lives because new economy jobs require experience and education, not muscles.

The report concluded that "from the point of view of public finances, Canada is probably the best equipped among [industrial] countries to face population aging. The dynamics of tax-deferred retirement savings plans should substantially reduce the negative pressure of aging on Canadian public savings by encouraging the shifting of taxable income well into the future when tax revenues will be most needed."

Besides, even if size does matter in Ottawa, Canada's massive demographic immigration experiment has arguably been a dud. A report in February 2002 revealed that even after the arrival of more than three million immigrants and refugees in 15 years, Canada's young families in 2000 were in less of a position than ever to look after the aging population. Young families in 1999 were significantly poorer than their 1985 counterparts. The average net worth of the country's 12.2 million families was $64,600, which represented a 10 percent increase since 1985. But couples between 25 and 34 years of age with children had only $30,800 in assets, one-third less than a decade before. Older families enjoyed an increase of 18 percent in asset value.

"We've been saying we should be concerned about it for years," commented a policy analyst with the Vanier Institute of the Family about this study. "This is the generation of people whose incomes and wealth will be required by that proportionately larger number of baby boomers once they've retired."

Statistics Canada agreed in its report and stated that the "sharp decline in net worth of young people with children during this 15-year period suggests that some may have relatively few financial assets to absorb the shock of economic stresses such as the loss of a job."

Ottawa's immigration influx has made the demographic situation worse. The average age of immigrants was 25 years between 1956 and 1976, but by 1994 had risen to 30 years. By 1997, immigrants comprised 18 percent of the country's population as a whole, but accounted for 28 percent of people older than 65 years of age. As policies now stand, the average immigration age will continue to rise because immigration officials are approving the entry of enough parents and grandparents as sponsored immigrants to replace a small town every year. Between 1998 and 2000, 46,420 elderly sponsored immigrants were let into the country, constituting 8 percent of all entrants during this period. In 2000, this represented 17,740 elderly persons out of 227,209 entrants.

Despite such a dismal demographic track record, Elinor Caplan, immigration minister until January 2002, continued to justify immigration practices on the basis of the demographic argument. At a Senate hearing in October 2001 into her proposed new legislation, which passed that December, she put forward her reasons for increasing immigration.

"We are already seeing skill shortages, and we know that immigrants bring buying power and prosperity. One does not have to do much more than drive around the larger urban centres to see the prosperity that immigrant communities have brought," she said. "We are growing older and having fewer children. More than three-quarters of Canada's labor force growth comes from immigration. In merely 10 years, immigration will count for all labor force growth in Canada. In merely 20 years, all of Canada's population growth will come from immigration. We must get the best and the brightest."

Obviously, the minister and her bureaucrats completely missed their own point. Her admission that the country faced a looming skills short-age—despite 15 years' worth of unprecedented immigration—should have been a damning indictment of Ottawa's selection process. Also damning was the growing evidence of the deteriorating economic performance of the newest immigrants, according to one study after another. Instead, she used that failure as an excuse to bring even more people into the country, mostly relatives of immigrants.

Besides letting in too many unqualified and elderly immigrants, Ottawa's immigration-cum-demographic policy had been wrongheaded to begin with. A 1989 report on demographics released by Health and Welfare Canada (based on 167 studies) showed that increased immigration would have a very limited impact on the dependency ratio (worker to retiree) problem. In 1998, the Department of Citizenship and Immigration released a report called *Immigration and Canadian Demographics*, which showed that doubling, or even tripling, the current levels of immigration would have little effect on the dependency ratio.

Daniel Stoffman, co-author of *Boom, Bust and Echo*, a book about Canada's demographic future, debunked the demographic mindset in an interview with me in the *National Post* in 2000. He said immigration is a useful economic tool only if productive or skilled people are allowed in and only if they do not displace existing workers. Then incomes rise for every-one. But that hasn't been the case. For instance, in British Columbia, which had a very large influx and attracted the wealthiest immigrants, per capita incomes have fallen steadily in the past 15 years.

If immigration was such a benefit, he added, then larger populations would always enjoy an economic benefit, and the biggest countries and biggest cities would be the most prosperous. The point was, he said, that there is no correlation between population size and population growth and economic well-being.

Canada's target figure of 250,000 was also arbitrary and unjustifiable given unemployment rates since the mid-1980s, he said. These immigration and refugee levels will greatly harm the 6.5 million Canadians born between 1980 and 1995, a demographic group known as the "Baby Boom Echo" generation. "Over the next decade, they will be moving into the job market and there will be unemployment and displacement problems at current immigration and refugee levels," he said.

Mr. Stoffman and his co-author, David Foot, said in their book that there was little reason to fear a shortage of working-age Canadians when the boomers retired. The Echo generation, like the Boom, constitutes a large population bulge.

Another study in 2001 by Statistics Canada questioned the demographic argument. It said that the population of the country would start to decline in several decades because even current high immigration levels would not offset low fertility levels. This is because immigrant birth rates change to match those of native-borns shortly after they arrive. And longevity for the entire population in the future would mean that the proportion of women in child-bearing years would decrease as time elapsed.

A United Nations' study in 2000 pointed out the same fundamental flaw in the "immigration can solve the aging population problem" argument. Canada was not included in the study, but the United States was and has a demographic age profile close to Canada's. Estimates were that the U.S. population would have to quadruple every 50 years to maintain the same demographic age because immigrants immediately take on the same aging and family-size characteristics as other Americans.

Statistics Canada estimated that if 60,000 immigrants arrived each year, roughly replacing the number who leave the country each year, the population would remain level until 2026. A journal called *The Demographic Review* indicated that, with net immigration of 80,000 per year, Canada should be able to maintain reasonable population levels in future.

Raymond Uhaldo, when he was U.S. Assistant Secretary of Labor, also pointed out the problem of counting on immigration to fix labor markets: "immigration fixes undercut efforts to improve public education, create better retraining programs and draw the unemployed into the labor market."

Likewise, the now-defunct Economic Council of Canada in 1991 questioned the benefits of immigration. "For much of Canada's history, it has been natural increase, not immigration, that has driven the growth of population. This conclusion casts considerable doubt on the proposition that history proves that Canada needs immigration. Only a few periodic bursts of immigration were needed—not sustained inflows. The same conclusion applies with respect to the country's economic prosperity: a historical perspective gives little or no support to the view that Canada needed immigration to become a wealthy nation."

Immigrants Don't Fill the Empty Spaces

Immigration between 1900 and 1910 populated the prairies, but most immigrants now head for Canada's three biggest cities, Toronto, Vancouver, and Montreal. They crowd into already congested urban areas where jobs, social services, and ethnic enclaves exist. At current rates of immigration, Toronto will have two million more persons to absorb in 15 years, and Vancouver one million. Statistics Canada in 2000 estimated that over the next 25 years, Canada's population will increase by five million persons, based on current fertility rates and immigration levels. This will mean even more people in those two cities.

Few Canadians, other than real-estate developers, think that would make any sense. Overpopulation will eliminate the quality of life in these cities, through higher real estate prices and congestion. High immigration levels will put further stress on already heavily burdened educational, health, and social welfare services by adding millions of newcomers who require support to adapt to life in Canada. There's also the issue of building new infrastructure to accommodate an explosion in population. Billions will be needed for roads, hospitals, public housing, schools, sewers, parks, recreation facilities, bridges, subways and buses, airports, and rail links.

In 2000, 74.3 percent of Canada's newcomers went to the three biggest cities: Toronto (47.55 percent), Vancouver (14.56 percent), and Montreal (12.3 percent). Another 8.67 percent went to three other cities: 3.71 percent to Calgary, 3.34 percent to Ottawa, and 1.62 percent to Winnipeg. Between 1991 and 1996, 93 percent ended up in cities. In its April 2000 report, the Canadian Council on Social Development noted that by 1996, 85 percent of all immigrants who ever came to Canada lived in cities.

The situation is identical south of the border. By 1998, 75 percent of all immigrants lived in six states—California, New York, Texas, Florida, New Jersey, and Illinois—where only one-third of native-borns lived. By the late 1990s, California hosted 32 percent of all immigrants. Another study in 1990 showed that 42 percent of immigrants lived in just five cities: New York, Los Angeles, Miami, Chicago, and Anaheim—where only 13 percent of native-born Americans lived. These cities also have the country's highest welfare entitlements and, as such, are known as "welfare magnets" for struggling immigrants.

Ethnic networks exist in these urban areas and provide members with information about how to tap into public housing, welfare, and health care or how to find a job, earn cash under the table, or commit crimes. As of 1990, nearly half of California's immigrants, particularly southeast Asian refugees, had been on welfare for years.

Welfare use by immigrants and refugees in Canada is also disproportionately high compared to that of the general population. In 2001, the City of Toronto had 8,000 refugees on welfare and 4,000 relatives whose sponsorships had "broken down." The annual cost, for all three levels of government, was roughly $120 million a year. In 1999, the mayor of Montreal estimated that one-third of all persons on welfare in his city were immigrants or refugees, and Mayor Phil Owen of Vancouver, in an interview in 2001, estimated that immigrant and refugee costs were "staggering" for taxpayers, especially if law enforcement expenses were included.

There are other "soft" costs attached to mass migration. A landmark study in 1995 by a Tulane University demographer, Leon Bouvier of the Federation for American Immigration Reform, examined life in cities with 7 percent immigrant populations and those with 25 percent or more. High immigration cities had "30 percent longer commuting times; 40 percent more people living in poverty; 60 percent more dropouts; twice as many violent crimes; twice the level of unemployment; twice the welfare dependency and seven times as much crowded housing." He called this the Misery Index and determined that large-scale immigration was behind the differences in quality of life.

The case against massive immigration levels has also been made by environmentalists. The arguments are interesting; however, they have predictably fallen on deaf ears in Ottawa. Representative was a paper called "Why Canada Needs a Population Policy," co-authored by Tony Cassils and Madeline Weld that was submitted to the Standing Committee on Citizenship and Immigration on May 1, 2001. Ms. Weld is a scientist with Health Canada. Mr. Cassils has been in law and finance and has been involved in promoting sustainable development.

"The idea that their country has a problem with overpopulation might strike most Canadians as preposterous. On the contrary, many see Canada as a vast empty land ripe for massive human settlement. Recent insights from the science of ecology, however, suggest that we greatly overestimate Canada's carrying capacity. The largely unchallenged assumption is that Canada has no population problem since it has the second largest land area of all countries on Earth. These unpopulated Canadian land areas are generally seen as "empty" spaces just waiting to be filled. These assumptions are based on a totally false premise that the potential for growth is equatable with the crude statistic of land area," they wrote.

"The reality is that much of the land is barren and incapable of supporting a large population. Furthermore, whatever population lived in these barren areas would leave a large 'ecological footprint.' Most food would have to be shipped in, requiring both land surface for agriculture elsewhere and large amounts of energy for transportation and space heating. The more habitable parts of Canada, the most southerly strip near the American border that is home to most Canadians, is already densely populated. Toronto and Vancouver are experiencing serious problems associated with their rapid, unplanned growth, yet Canada continues to actively seek large numbers of immigrants who gravitate towards these regions. Anyone using the Lions Gate Bridge in Vancouver, Highway 401 in southern Ontario, or emergency services at hospitals across the country, knows that we do not lack people," they added.

"Transplanting population from low-consuming regions to high-consuming ones merely accelerates the deterioration of the planet. Yet over the past decade, Canada has accepted about 250,000 people a year as immigrants and refugees or as illegal economic migrants, with about half of them coming from very poor regions. Given Canadian levels of consumption, the effect on the Earth is equivalent to adding 7.5 to 12.5 million extra people annually in a poor country [because they will consume more in Canada]. Also its goal to vastly increase immigration levels would appear to be at odds with the objective of reducing greenhouse gas emissions."

Family Reunification Problems

Former Immigration Minister Elinor Caplan liked to describe family reunification privileges as the "cornerstone of the country's immigration system." Traditionally, immigration has been about strong young men coming to Canada to work. Some brought wives and children, but distant relatives had to come on their own merit. After 1986, this changed. What also has changed is that in the past, reunification was permitted if landed immigrants could afford to support those relatives. Such sponsorships were a tradeoff. In return for permission to bring relatives into the country, sponsors had to agree to support them for at least 10 years so that they would not become a burden on Canadian taxpayers.

But that is no longer true. The minute relatives arrive they are liable to become a burden to the welfare state. This is because sponsorship does not go far enough and also because the federal government has failed to enforce these agreements. Sponsors are often not properly researched for financial capability. Others simply renege but are allowed to get away with it because Ottawa never chases deadbeat sponsors, leaving taxpayers on the hook to provide assistance.

As noted, *Bill C-11* has made the ability to reunite distant relatives, and even love-interests, easier. Once arrived, even sponsored immigrants can, in turn, sponsor. In other words, a "dependent" child 22 years old can be brought into Canada and can immediately sponsor other people.

With such an open-ended scheme, in a highly advanced economy, it's little wonder that poverty levels are increasing for immigrants. If they are totally unskilled and without English or French, they would be unable to earn even a minimum wage, condemning them to chronic unemployment or welfare for years. That reality for many, plus group living, has led to the creation of a culture of welfarism. One Immigration spokesperson guessed that at least 10 percent of sponsors default, causing many sponsored relatives to go on assistance.

The federal government has not properly devised a system to prevent defaults. In April 1999, I was leaked a document by an immigration official that revealed how Ottawa's immigration department had not been properly checking the finances of sponsoring immigrants to ensure that they could support the persons they pledged to support. The report was done by an Immigration official named Alain Gingras and was widely circulated throughout the department. My source, who asked to remain anonymous, said its conclusions had fallen on deaf ears, but pointed out a frightening problem.

Mr. Gingras circulated a random questionnaire to Sri Lankan sponsors. He found that 40 percent of a sampling of sponsors approved to bring a relative into Canada did not meet any of the financial criteria required of them to support their relative. This was due to the insufficient and inept investigation of their financial assets and incomes. He also concluded that the same problem applied to all sponsors from all ethnic groups.

In his report's preamble, Mr. Gingras stated that he felt the survey was needed because he had seen abuses of the system while he had been a visa officer in Sri Lanka from 1996 to 1998. People sneaking into Canada under false pretenses, pretending they were landed immigrants in order to become fake refugees, was such a problem that anyone flying to Canada first had to appear at the Canadian High Commission in Colombo, Sri Lanka, to have their documents checked and to be interviewed in order to make sure they were *bona fide* Canadian permanent residents. During this time Mr. Gingras inspected and interviewed thousands of these people and was shocked to find that the majority of them who were living in Canada had been sponsored and yet had been living for years on welfare.

"When I asked them why their sponsors were not supporting them, they generally replied that the sponsors did not have the financial means to do so," he said.

His study consisted of sending out separate surveys to 247 sponsors that asked for more detailed information than the federal government had asked during its approval process. For instance, he asked sponsors for three years' income history, not just one year as was required. He also asked those applying to sponsor spouses and children for evidence of their income. Canadian Immigration officials do not require evidence when it involves immediate family, only for more distant relatives. They also did not ask for the appropriate documents and accepted unreliable sources as evidence. Mr. Gingras also asked sponsors to provide him with a family tree so he could determine how many people the sponsor had to support already. Immigration officials never did this.

His overall results were as follows: Some 99 sponsors (40 percent) did not have the financial means to support the sponsored person; 93 sponsors (38 percent) did have the means; 35 sponsors (14 percent) did not respond or responded in such a way that it was impossible to form an opinion; and 20 sponsors (8 percent) refused to cooperate.

He concluded that the fact that the federal government required less information about sponsorship for closer relatives guaranteed more failures. For instance, he found that 34 percent of the 98 sponsors who were approved to bring in parents, grandparents, and fiancés were incapable of supporting them. But the figure was much higher when it came to those 39 sponsors who were approved to bring in spouses and dependent children; some 59 percent could not support them.

He blamed the fact that evaluation was based on insufficient information. Would-be sponsors were given a choice as to how they proved their income. They could merely bring in employer letters, paycheque stubs, income tax returns, T4s, or Revenue Canada notices of assessment. "There is no doubt that sponsors supply documents that are to their advantage in some cases, [hiding business expenses if self-employed, for example]. It is more than likely that some sponsors present flagrantly fraudulent documents [falsified letters of employment, T4s produced fraudulently, fake income tax returns]. I think this is what explains the 34 percent 'error' rate," Mr. Gingras wrote in the report.

For instance, a taxi driver could claim to have an income of $40,000, but his expenses may be $20,000, thus putting his income level too low to sponsor. But full and complete information might never be sought by Immigration Canada officials. Another problem is that a relative or accomplice could pose as an employer and write a letter or provide a phoney T4 slip. Mr. Gingras said that the only *bona fide* document proving income levels was a Revenue Canada Notice of Assessment, because these documents are difficult to counterfeit. They show both taxes paid and taxable income.

But even if a sponsor has sufficient income, the department might also fail to take into account the fact that the sponsor may already have a large family to support on that money, thus putting his remaining income level too low to sponsor others, said the Gingras report. (I interviewed a Somalian cab driver in Toronto with an income of only $20,000 per year who was able to sponsor 35 relatives, none of whom he could support. All were in public housing and on welfare.)

Mr. Gingras's study zeroed in on Sri Lankans because of his professional experiences in the field as a visa officer there.

"Thirty-four percent of Sri Lankan sponsors who are approved are, in fact, incapable of supporting the sponsored persons. Can this proportion be extended to sponsors of other nationalities?" he asked in the report. "There is no reason to think that sponsors of any other national origin have a different experience. We can therefore reasonably presume that approximately 34 percent of all sponsors approved do not, in fact, have the means to sponsor."

But the fact is that no one knows and, even though his report certainly raised some red flags, the federal government has never undertaken any analysis to determine the drain on taxpayers. All that a sponsored immigrant in Canada need do is to show up at a welfare office and have his sponsor swear an affidavit that he or she cannot, or will not, support him or her any longer. Then the immigrant is automatically entitled to benefits.

Ottawa's Downloading Games

The result of sponsorship "breakdown" has been undue hardship to taxpayers. Every month since November 1990, feisty Mississauga Mayor Hazel McCallion and her region's government have sent the federal government an invoice for that 20 percent portion of the welfare payments that the region has had to pay for refugees and sponsored immigrants whose sponsors weren't meeting their financial obligations. Peel Region comprises 900,000 people living in Mississauga, Brampton, and Caledon. The cumulative cost to the region's taxpayers, from November 1990 to March 2001, reached $26,733,260 by the end of 2000.

"That is comprised of $10,740,620 of social assistance costs and $15,992,640 in accrued interest," wrote David Szwarc, interim commissioner of Peel Social Services in a report. "In 2000, the Region of Peel issued assistance to 658 refugee claimant cases each month. That is 8.2 percent of the monthly cases issued assistance for that year."

Another 11.3 percent of the region's caseload is due to "sponsorship breakdown."

Mr. Swarc continues, "These are immigrants who were sponsored to Canada for a period of 10 years by their relatives. However, those relatives stop supporting them and they apply for financial assistance," wrote Mr. Szwarc. "We attempt to contact the sponsoring family member and remind them of their obligation to support, but we have no authority to compel them to resume their obligation. The federal government's own immigration legislation does not give it the authority to compel the sponsor to resume support either. All the federal legislation allows the Immigration Department to do is to take the defaulting sponsor to court to collect the social assistance that was paid, and/or to prevent the sponsor from sponsoring any more immigrants until the debt has been repaid," he wrote. "In 2000, the Region of Peel issued assistance to 908 sponsorship breakdown cases each month. That is 11.3 percent of the monthly cases issued assistance for that year."

In other words, refugee claimant and sponsorship breakdown cases represented nearly 20 percent of the caseload in Peel Region, a disproportionate percentage. The cost to Peel, however, represented only 20 percent of the total cost of welfare. The other two levels of government, the provincial and federal governments, paid the rest directly and indirectly. This meant that the welfare costs of refugee claimants and sponsored immigrants in Peel alone totalled $13 million a year.

Toronto has greater problems because it receives about 47 percent of all immigrants and refugees in the country. Its facilities have been stretched to the limit because of the influx. In 1999, the tab for temporary shelters or motel rooms for hundreds of refugee claimants was $1.9 million per month. Public health expenditures for refugee claimants alone in the city were $3 million per year, not including the $12 million contributed by the province. In terms of welfare, on average in 2001 there were 8,000 welfare cases involving refugees at any given time and up to 5,000 sponsorship breakdown immigration cases.

Toronto's outspoken Mayor Mel Lastman said the city's taxpayers must spend inordinate amounts of money on immigration and refugee expenses. And he spends an excessive amount of time fighting with the federal government to help it realize it should defray the cost of its immigration.

"It's costing us $30 million a year every year. We are stuck with all the bills, welfare, health care, crime issues, court cases, and we have no say over who gets in here. The feds let in refugees and don't even know where they are and who they are," he said. "We have to pay for hotel rooms for refugees from Oshawa to Niagara Falls. Ottawa takes billions from this city in taxes and doesn't give back. I met with the prime minister and he agreed it's terrible. He says he'll look into it and does nothing."

After the 9–11 terrorist attacks, the mayor said federal law enforcement officials asked local police to round up suspects or check out the identities and whereabouts of refugees suspected of terrorist links who had gone missing.

"The feds don't even know whether these people are terrorists. It cost $1 million for us to try to find these people who are terrorists. They let these people in and we have to police them. It's simply ridiculous," he said.

In 1995–96, a pilot program in Peel to get deadbeat sponsors to support their family members was undertaken by federal immigration officials and was successful. "It was labor intensive and involved federal immigration officers calling these deadbeat sponsors in to remind them they were sponsors and they should get their family members off welfare. It worked. But then the feds refused to do that [i.e., they stopped]," said John Baird, Ontario Minister of Community and Social Services in an interview in spring 2002. Another experiment by several provinces in 1999 involved suing 1,600 deadbeat sponsors with the permission of the federal government. But the lawsuits were abandoned without explanation.

By 2002, the annual deadbeat bill for welfare in Ontario alone was $150 million a year. Ontario is trying to force Ottawa to change rules to stop the problem or to compensate the lower levels of government. "What bothers me the most is the sponsorship defaults. We now have 16,000 cases in Ontario. The sponsor is a deadbeat, and the federal government is an enabler. People who sponsor should have to put up a bond. And there was widespread support for that suggestion, but nothing happens," said Mr. Baird.

"The overwhelming majority of these cases are in Toronto, Peel, and Ottawa. The cause is simple: The federal government sets the criteria and does not hold the sponsor accountable. It bothers me: Why should we have to go after 16,000 people?" said Mr. Baird. "Where's the social justice in letting some deadbeat off the hook? I just don't get it."

Ontario and Ottawa shared the cost of an ambitious report into sponsorship breakdown and other immigration issues. The finding was that the problem did not surface for the first three years after sponsored family members arrived in Canada, but welfare problems occurred thereafter. So, ironically, Ottawa incorporated a change in the *Immigration Act* in 2001 that reduces the sponsorship requirement to only three years instead of 10.

"So they just unload the problem immediately by reducing the requirement and load it onto our backs. That's the last study I'll do with the feds on this. It just gives them ideas as to how to back away," said Mr. Baird. "Under the new act, there is a provision that we can legally collect from sponsors. But this is to be done through garnishees of wages. This means we would have to go to court each and every time. That would cost a fortune and is simply because the feds haven't taken responsibility," he said.

Worse yet, the federal government is approving sponsors who are already on welfare themselves or getting disability assistance.

"Under *Bill C-11* you can be a deadbeat sponsor and sponsor someone else. Allowing people on welfare or people with disabilities to sponsor someone is just absurd. Think about it: The federal government has a sponsor sign a paper which guarantees their sponsored immigrant will not go on social assistance when the sponsor himself or herself is already on social assistance. It's crazy," said the minister. "You have a person on disability getting $920 a month, and who has less than $5,000 in assets. They cannot, by definition, support themselves, and the feds let them sponsor someone else? How can they say they can take care of somebody else? The simple solution is for us to say they are ineligible."

Ontario has sought legal advice to see whether it can sue the federal government to recoup such costs, but was told that it was constitutionally impossible. Besides welfare expenses imposed on provinces and municipalities, Ottawa's immigration practices impose unknown medical, educational, justice, or housing costs on these lower levels. Even worse, the feds are advertising these entitlements.

"They're advertising our welfare system on the worldwide web. Imagine that? How much is that costing us all? We have no breakdown of the medical or educational costs. We know that Quebec accepts anyone, and a year later they end up in Toronto from Montreal needing English as a Second Language and social assistance. We know that legal aid costs are going through the roof because of refugee claims," he said. "And when the feds allow them to bring in their elderly parents or grandparents, who are sponsored because they are not entitled to old age security, they make me give them welfare."

Fortunately, all able-bodied welfare recipients in Ontario must enroll in one of three programs, which has cut down abuses: Workfare requires 17 hours of work a week in public services and a job search; Earnfare requires part-time work with welfare making up the difference; and Learnfare requires recipients to attend school to upgrade their job skills. Disabled persons and those with preschool children are exempt from these require-ments. Since 1995, the welfare rolls have shrunk by 60 percent. Alberta has had the same experience. Quebec refuses to give welfare to sponsored immigrants, so they go to Ontario.

Ontario also instituted a "zero tolerance" policy when it comes to welfare cheats, and instituted a hotline and hired 100 investigators. In addi-tion, recipients' credit card expenditures, car registrations, student loans, and other financial arrangements are reviewed to note whether there is illicit outside income or unusually extravagant expenditures, he said.

While Ontario and others impose new discipline on their spending programs, Ottawa's new *Immigration Act* will facilitate abuses. The latest legislation permits anyone to sponsor a common-law "partner" (homosexual or heterosexual) of only one year. "This means that those wanting to get in here won't even have to do the fake marriage scam anymore," he said. "This is elitism gone crazy. It's about political correctness and the disconnect between the policy and the payer. There's a huge gap. We have deadbeat spon-sors that are costing $150 million or more each year in this province. What a huge difference that $150 million would make for agencies dealing with Down's Syndrome youngsters or disabled ones, suicidal children, dysfunc-tional families, shelters for battered women, autistic kids? Think how many textbooks that would buy? Or nurses that would employ? It's obscene."

Exact education costs are also unknown. About 400,000 immigrant children have arrived in 15 years, at a cost per year of $800 million to school boards. Then there is the cost of language instruction, plus adult education to upgrade the skills of refugees and sponsored adults.

Donna Cansfield, chairwoman of the Toronto Public School Board, said immigration and refugee children are a huge burden on her board, which is North America's fourth-largest school system, with 270,000 kids and 30,000 teachers and other workers. Nearly one-third, or 82,800 out of the 270,000 school population, between junior kindergarten and Grade 12, were born outside Canada. The birthplace of another 22,944, or 7.8 percent of the total, is unknown.

This escalates the cost of education greatly. The Toronto Board is spending $62.5 million per year to provide support services for refugee and immigrant students through intake and settlement offices staffed by community advisors, social workers, interpreters, and "intake workers." Then there are the English as a Second Language tutoring costs, which amount to $51 million per year. That brings the total immigration/ refugee-related taxpayer cost to $113.5 million plus another $20 million or so borne by the separate, or Roman Catholic, school system in Toronto. Worst of all, the boards are having to divert money from other students to support these special services because provinces are unwilling to give extra funds for resettlement costs, and the federal government, even though it is in charge of immigration, deflects fiscal responsibility by saying that education is a provincial matter. "We're caught in the middle without help," said Mrs. Cansfield.

A bigger burden on taxpayers is health care. The three million immigrants allowed into Canada between 1986 and 2000 represent a tab of roughly $6.9 billion a year (average health care cost is $2,300 per person per year). Welfare entitlements could run another $300 million annually based on Ontario's figures. Then there are the unknown costs of providing housing, disability pensions, and administration. Unlike immigration of old, every newcomer to a welfare state is a huge potential cost unless he or she can generate a great deal of income and tax dollars.

Downloading costs was an issue addressed before the Senate by Mayor Anne Mulvale from the Town of Oakville, Ontario. An immigrant herself, she is president of the Association of Municipalities of Ontario (AMO) and a member of the board of the Federation of Canadian Municipalities (FCM), which is the national voice of Canada's 5,000 municipal governments. The AMO represents almost all of Ontario's 447 municipal governments, and 98 percent of Ontario's population. The FCM director, John Burrett, spoke first to the senators:

"We do believe that our communities need to be protected and kept safe from those who are not here for the good of the country [terrorists or criminals] or the good of local communities. All government officials need to work closer together to ensure the safety of Canadians. All three orders of government and the respective law enforcement agencies need to re-examine how they coordinate their efforts effectively," he said.

"Second, across Canada we have a shortage of skilled workers in our health care system, in our schools and in the technology sector, and in many other areas. If we and our cities are to compete globally to sustain and expand our economic well-being, we need to develop multifaceted plans to deal with this shortage. We clearly support the principles of refugee protection first by saving lives and taking into account the best interests of children. Having said that, however, we do need to look at how best to support the variety of assistance that newcomers need. If we cannot deliver on those supports, whether it be housing, dental care, training, or income assistance, then we are not doing justice to public policy or public service," he said.

Mayor Mulvale bemoaned the use of property taxes to pay for services resulting from federal immigration policies.

"Municipal government is the order of government at the bottom of the financial food chain. However, this should not and must not be used as the default funding mechanism for a federal policy program or for a provincial policy program. There should not be a distinction or disconnect between the order of government that develops the policy and the order of government that pays to implement the policy. Simply put, the financial component for the programs needed to support Canada's immigration policies should not be funded in whole or in part by the property tax base. But rather, it should be funded by the federal government. Why? The reason is that there is a flawed assumption that the property tax owner has the capacity to pay. In Ontario, property taxes are based on the market value of the property, not on personal or corporate income. Property taxes are paid with after-tax dollars. Those are more expensive dollars to the spender," she said.

"Property taxes were never meant to support social programs, but rather to support policing, fire, and waste disposal. Federal tax dollars should be devoted to federal policies. We need to return to this basic premise and work with the federal government on a funding program for those social and community health programs that are needed to support immigrants and refugees. Why is this of paramount importance to Ontario's municipalities? Let us look at some of the statistics. In summary, today's immigrants are older on average, and women make up the majority of immigrant seniors. Recent immigrants are less likely to speak either official language, as compared to immigrants who have lived in Canada for longer periods. Recent immigrants are somewhat less likely to be part of the paid workforce, as compared to their non-immigrant counterparts. Recent immigrants were more likely to be unemployed—19 percent as compared to earlier-arriving counterparts at 9 percent," she said.

Ontario's cities must bear inordinately high expenses because of the increase in numbers plus the fact that recent immigrants are older, poorer, work less, and speak French and English less frequently than the previous immigrants, she said. Ontario gets $864 per immigrant arrival from Ottawa, which does not compare well with other provinces. For example, Quebec gets $3,252 per immigrant arrival. These funds are not spread around fairly because of favoritism.

"To show you the impact in London, every additional 1,000 social assistance cases means close to $1.5 million in added costs. There are thousands of cases of immigrants receiving social assistance because of sponsorship breakdown and refugee claimants who need to be accommodated in emergency shelters. It is clear that Ontario municipalities are facing tremendous increased financial pressures to meet the social, economic and safety impact of newcomers. What is needed? An understanding of the impact of immigrants and refugees on the local community and supporting the local community's climate of welcome. We agree that newcomers bring social, cultural, and economic benefit to our communities," she said.

"With benefits come some challenges. One challenge is that government, education, social, health, cultural, and economic institutions have to adapt to the growing diversity in the population. Municipalities have and will continue to develop strategies to create a positive climate of welcome to newcomers. Municipalities have and will continue to strengthen respect among residents for diversity. The local community also has to respond to the health, educational, and social service needs of refugees and immigrants who experience difficulties, especially during the initial period of settlement.

"The federal government should support the funding of programs and initiatives for the successful integration of immigrants and refugees. Examples of programs and initiatives that will facilitate settlement include public awareness and education on the benefit of immigration, English as second language training, access to schooling for newcomer children, access and equitable settlement services, affordable housing strategies, skills upgrades for foreign trade workers, and collaboration with provincial regulation bodies and technical associations to accelerate the recognition and certification of foreign credentials."

The federal government should reimburse other levels for all expenses incurred from public health costs to welfare, hostels, and other costs such as language training. "It really is a matter of stopping the downloading. It will not serve the federal policy related to immigrants and refugees if municipal governments have to increase property tax or cut other municipal services to finance the related increased costs. This is not how to support the federal immigration or refugee policy."

Health Care Concerns

In 2000, a handwritten sign was taped to a wall in the emergency room of Toronto's Wellesley Hospital, which read: "Last year, we treated 13,000 refugees in this emergency." Ironically, the hospital was closed one year later because of the burgeoning health care budget in the province.

One of Canada's most revered social services is health care. The cost of health care for the 210,000 parents and grandparents allowed into the country since 1986, if still alive, would amount to $1.69 billion per year alone. Every year, visitors to Canada arrive pregnant in order to give birth in hospitals and to claim citizenship for their children. In France, by contrast, citizenship is not automatically granted to a child born in that country; a residency requirement must be fulfilled in adulthood.

There is also a public health issue. One upsetting example I wrote about in 1999 involved Vancouver physician Maria Hugi, who was exposed to tuberculosis (TB) from a Burmese refugee she treated in a hospital, who also had full-blown AIDS. Dr. Hugi was a victim of the fact that refugees are never detained for medical examination.

"My dog has more protection at the border than I do. Pets are quarantined so that our dogs don't get dog diseases," said Dr. Hugi. "We quarantine birds, horses. Anything green that comes across the border cannot come right into Canada. The government, when it comes to protecting our pets and livestock and plants, does a real efficient job. To me as a physician, a life form is a life form, and you should do the same thing with people. You screen and quarantine. They [the government border officials] do a good job of protecting us from imported disease when it involves life forms that can't talk. But when it comes to illegal aliens, the immigration and refugee lawyers—who need to finance their children's orthodontics and to buy fancy houses with big fees—corrupt the system."

Dr. Hugi is also an immigrant who came at the age of three from Switzerland with her parents. Ironically, her family's application was held up for three years because her father had a spot on his lung and authorities made him get further X-rays to show that his condition had not deteriorated.

"This is fine and understandable and we now require health reports on immigrants. But refugees are a totally different situation," she said.

She treated the man in the emergency ward of Mount St. Joseph Hospital in Vancouver in May 1998. He had stopped breathing. "I ran into the room, and there was pandemonium. People are running for the equipment. You don't have time to look at the charts and must make a decision what to do, so you rely on the nurses to tell you the story. The first thing I saw was a young Asian man. I asked how old? Twenty-six. What's the deal, he looks thin? What sort of disease? Why's he here? The only thing they could tell me is that he'd been in the country eight months, and he was a refugee from Burma. I assumed that he'd be screened for everything. That would be what our government did and the responsible thing to do. I remember my father's story," she said.

"I resuscitated him, put a tube in through his mouth and into his lungs and brought him back to life," she recalled. "I transferred him to the ICU [Intensive Care Unit] where he spent two weeks before he died. I turned him over to an internist who assumed his care. I ran into that doctor and asked what happened. I was certain he died. He told me he had full-blown AIDS. I didn't worry about that because we're careful about that and I didn't come into contact with his blood. But the next thing hit me right in the solar plexis and he told me that the guy had full-blown TB. I sort of fell against the wall."

"I waited three months [it takes that long to be determined] and was sweating bullets because he had full-blown AIDS, and I was worried about exposure to a certain kind of TB. If a person from Burma has AIDS, he may have this multiple-drug-resistant TB, which usually comes from southeast Asia. Fortunately, his TB was not the TB that resists drugs. So I went on this medication," she said.

"TB is a very complex disease. Once your skin test is positive, it doesn't mean it's in your lungs. Your immune system is still developing a response. You have a 15 percent chance it will get into your lungs and kill you. The clincher about INH [the drug she's taken to combat TB] is that it gives the liver a real workout for anyone over 30, and I'm 46. INH can kill the liver. I was annoyed because I knew I had to take something that's pretty toxic. So far, my liver is still functioning according to tests, but it's small comfort that you have to give up 60 percent of your liver before it shows up in testing."

She wrote to Immigration Minister Lucienne Robillard twice about the recklessness of the system before getting any response. "I got a letter saying it was my fault for being in a high-risk profession and everything's hunky dory with our system," she said. "That was insulting. I have no quarrel with looking after a Canadian, a homeless person. That's my social contract. But I expect the government to protect us from foreign invasion. That's the skinny. If we didn't think that way, then let's just stop pretending and eliminate the border."

She also worried about immigrant examinations conducted abroad.

"These exams can be bought on the black market in countries, so can chest X-rays. The system should require that an immigrant applicant be examined by a Canadian doctor working with equipment from here."

Outbreaks of Third World diseases began to crop up across Canada due to the inadequate public health screening procedures. Toronto reported 180 cases of leprosy among men from India or Southeast Asia in 1999—the highest caseload in the Western world of this disease, which is spread by discharge of the nasal lining. TB diagnoses have resulted in thousands of

Canadians having to be tested because of exposure to fellow students, workers, or neighbors.

In 1999, Dr. David McKeown, Toronto's medical officer, said 78 percent of TB cases involved foreign-born persons, because many immigrants from countries in which TB is rife have descended upon the city. These include mostly Asian, African, Latin American and Eastern European countries. Ninety-two percent of the 450 TB cases reported in 1998 were immigrants who were exposed to the disease in their former country, according to the Ontario Medical Association. Montreal had the same problem.

"The infection rate among foreign-born residents under the age of 30 is 20 times that of Canadian-born residents. People from outside of Canada accounted for 77 percent of TB cases in Montreal, although only 23 percent of the population is foreign-born," said Dr. Terry Tannenbaum, a Montreal public health researcher. Hepatitis B, epidemic in Asia, has also been brought into Canada by immigrants and refugees.

Sometimes Ottawa knowingly allowed people into the country with diseases that would cost taxpayers millions to treat. In 2000, Ottawa accepted 200 refugee claimants with AIDS and more than 500 with non-treatable tuberculosis. Treatments cost our health care system millions per patient. In December 2001, an outbreak of non-treatable tuberculosis occurred in Toronto hostels and drop-in centres frequented by refugee claimants. Two of the 14 people diagnosed in these facilities died. The year before, there were 376 isolated cases of active TB in Toronto, all traced back to new immigrants, said Sharon Pollack, TB manager for the health unit.

The public health risk has been neglected by Ottawa, and an immigrant allowed in with a deadly strain of tuberculosis launched a $500 million class action lawsuit against the government in 2000 for wrongly allowing him into the country. Gaspare Benjamin, a 37-year-old singer who immigrated in 1999 from the Dominican Republic, is suing along with his Canadian wife and friends, all of whom were infected by Mr. Benjamin. His lawyer said he hopes the 92 people who were possibly infected by him, and another

1,500 potentially exposed, will join the action. The federal government, two doctors working for Citizenship and Immigration Canada, and a local family physician are named in the suit.

"I think all of them share a sense of outrage," said the lawyer. "They were infected and they shouldn't have been. We want to make sure it doesn't happen again."

A notice of action, filed on December 18, 2000, states that the defendants "knew or ought to have known [Mr. Benjamin] would be a danger to public health" and his illness could "cause excessive demands on health or social services." An estimated $1.3 million alone was spent by Hamilton health authorities to track down those exposed to his disease. The cost to taxpayers of care for all those infected now and in the future will run to millions. Mr. Benjamin was examined by Immigration-approved doctors in the Dominican Republic before he came here. His case illustrated how inept the screening process is and how immigration and refugee procedures represent a public health hazard.

Will the Children Do Better?

At a cocktail party before the annual Public Policy Forum dinner in Toronto in 2001, the prime minister's then-chief of staff and top civil servant, Mel Cappe, and I had a brief, but telling, conversation. I complained to him about the struggling immigrants and refugees we were allowing into Canada and the effect this was having on the country. Mr. Cappe responded, "But their children will do well."

That is unsupported. Mr. Cappe's forebears were probably among those who came in the first or second waves from Europe, and were educated, skilled, and acculturated. Even if they were unskilled, they were entering an economy that required their manual labor. If immediate employment was unavailable, they went home or emigrated to the United States. They were never an expense to the country because there was no social safety net except one's family members or charities.

The difference now is that Canada, and the United States to a lesser extent, has been importing mostly unskilled labor from the Third World despite the complete economic restructuring that has occurred. This means education matters, and it matters a lot. For instance, uneducated immigrants in the past found jobs in manufacturing. But these jobs no longer exist. Only 15 percent of American workers and 18 percent of Canadian workers are employed in factories, half as many as after the Second World War. These workers are highly trained and highly paid. Farm jobs no longer exist either, except seasonally and at very low wages.

The only labor-intensive services that are growing employ highly skilled "knowledge workers" who must have the languages, adaptability, and education to improve professionally. Canada does not need more parking lot attendants, dishwashers, housekeepers, or cab drivers, but that's the skill level of many who came in the 1990s. The labor mismatch, and low education levels of most entrants (twice as many immigrants have less than Grade 9 education as do native-borns), is why it is less likely now for the performances of their children to improve in the future. Most will live in economic-ethnic ghettoes for generations and remain members of their underclass. Dropout rates for the children of immigrants are higher than for native-borns, according to inner-city statistics in Toronto.

"We cannot keep the kids in high school because they either hate it, because they struggle with the curriculum, or else they have to work to help support the extended family, or they have absolutely no ambition," said an exasperated secondary school principal in downtown Toronto. "In other cases, it's a cultural thing. Everybody is a cleaning lady or everybody grows marijuana indoors or everybody in their ethnic group is a laborer. That's all they aspire to be or that's all they are capable of doing."

Another impediment is the sheer number of arrivals. Enclaves of certain ethnic groups, who have taken the most advantage of family reunification rules, have formed in Toronto, Vancouver, and Montreal. These groups have little reason, or incentive, to assimilate. And if they don't assimilate, they cannot achieve. Many don't learn English. Their attitudes are often impediments to social advancement. "National origin matters in terms of success. Ethnicity matters and for a long time," said economist Professor Borjas in his book *Heaven's Door*.

In Ontario, for instance, huge numbers of Chinese children, even those born here or raised by their grandparents or other caregivers speaking Mandarin only, are hitting the school system and don't qualify for English as a Second Language tutoring because they have been more than two years in the country or were born here. That means funds from other students must be streamed, if at all possible, into their tutoring. Even if tutored for a short period of time, the child's success will be sandbagged from the get-go because of poor language skills.

Toronto school board chair Donna Cansfield said that dropout rates among immigrant and refugee children, indicators of future success, are horrific among certain ethnic groups. The board tracks such figures and has found that many cultures simply do not value education. Dropout rates are high for children who are disadvantaged because they come from dysfunctional or fragmented families, or because they cannot master Canada's culture, make friends, or finish schoolwork.

"Immigration and the lack of resources to help assimilate these kids has been a concern of mine for a long time. Everybody acknowledges the problem and nobody takes responsibility for it," she said. "Immigration is one of the greatest challenges we have as a school board. They are literally flooding into Toronto. How does a teacher cope with four different languages in her classroom? It is not unusual for one classroom of 25 to have 16 kids who did not speak any English. In one school in Islington there are 64 languages spoken by the students," she said.

The adolescent immigrant finds adjustment particularly difficult.

"In secondary school it's worse because you have to throw in hormones, peer group pressures, disposable income for extracurricular activities, dress competition, wanting to fit in, money problems, and cultural issues for some of them like the Muslim girls," she said.

Dropout rates are horrendous for kids who come to Canada as older children but who are illiterate or cannot speak any English or French. They are put into segregated classrooms for two years to learn English and upgrade, but often this treatment is stigmatizing, thus souring them on the education and socializing process altogether.

"The norm among African Canadians [Somalians, Ghanians, and others] is to feel their kids can't learn, and there are no expectations. Caribbean kids have a similar problem. The dropout rates for these groups are huge. It's very, very concerning and when you first see them it makes you ill," she said. "Another group are Portuguese kids, and the sense of low self-esteem about learning perpetuates itself within the community to the third and fourth generation. It's not about IQ or language. It's about the six inches in between their ears."

In the 1950s, two-thirds of legal immigrants to the U.S. were educated and from Europe or Canada. One-quarter were from Latin America and 6 percent from Asia. By the 1990s, only 17 percent of immigrants came from Europe or Canada, with 50 percent from Latin America and 30 percent from Asia. In Canada, in 1961, only 3 percent of immigrants came from the Middle East and Asia. Now 48 percent do. Between 1998 and 2000, the top 10 source countries in terms of Canadian immigration had become China (which went from 11 percent of immigrants and refugees to 16 percent), India (8.83 percent to 11.47 percent), Pakistan (4.65 percent to 6.24 percent), the Philippines (4.7 percent to 4.4 percent), Korea (2.82 percent to 3.36 percent), Sri Lanka (1.91 percent to 2.57 percent), the U.S. (from 2.74 percent to 2.56 percent), Iran (1.89 percent to 2.47 percent), Yugoslavia (0.67 percent to 2.08 percent), and the United Kingdom (2.24 percent to 2.05 percent). The top 10 represent half of the 591,282 who arrived during those three years.

Wage comparisons tell the story. For instance, a Somalian laborer in Canada makes 70 percent less than an American, South African, or European immigrant living here. Studies show his children will fare worse, typical for Third World migrants. In fact, Professor Borjas found that the children of all immigrants rarely outperform their parents. For instance, he said a Canadian immigrant to the U.S. in 1970 made 21 percent more than an American whose grandparents had immigrated. That Canadian immigrant's offspring made only 16 percent more than native-borns whose grandparents had immigrated. For unskilled persons the deterioration was far worse. Filipino immigrants in 1970 made 12.9 percent less than third-generation Americans, and two generations later, in 1998, their children made 17 percent less. Mexicans, Indians, and Haitians deteriorated as generations passed.

This is because, Professor Borjas said, the children of recent unskilled, uneducated immigrants improve their skills, and therefore wage levels, glacially. This means, in our fast-moving modern economies, they end up losing ground despite slight improvements. He estimated that the gap in skills between immigrants and native-borns is cut in half roughly every generation, or every 20 years. This means if there is a 20 percent wage gap in the first generation, there will be a 10 percent in the second and 5 percent in the third. For instance, in 1990 a Canadian immigrant to the United States earned twice as much as a Mexican immigrant. Using the findings, this means that even the grandchildren of a Canadian immigrant will still earn more than the grandchildren of the Mexican immigrant.

In other words, it could take more than 80 years for immigrant prosperity to even out or match that of native-borns in the New Economy. The ethnic groups may also become immersed in a welfare culture—thanks to the welfare state—which tends to slow down, or eliminate, any improvements. And Professor Borjas said there is proof of welfare use passed down from generation to generation.

"The intergenerational correlation in welfare use is far stronger than the intergenerational correlation in educational attainment or wages," wrote

Professor Borjas. "We call it the 'intergenerational stickiness of welfare use.' This strong intergenerational link in welfare use indicates a long-run fiscal burden on taxpayers who reside in the main immigrant-receiving states."

Professor Borjas, himself a Cuban immigrant to the United States, talked about another influence he dubbed "ethnic capital."

"A person's ethnic background—in and of itself—influences the process of social mobility. In particular, the skills of the next generation depend not only on what parents do but also on the characteristics of the ethnic environment where the children are raised," he said. "For better or worse, the interactions between residential segregation and ethnic capital generate a recurring cycle. Ethnic influences, both good and bad, play the same role generation after generation. If, through the accident of birth, one happens to be born into a disadvantaged ethnic group, the cycle is vicious; it is hard to escape the economic fate implied by one's ethnic background, and the children in these groups will often experience poor socioeconomic achievements. If, however, one happens to be born into an advantaged ethnic group, the cycle is virtuous: it is also hard to escape one's ethnic fate, but the children of this group are instead sentenced to a life of economic privilege."

One of the greatest issues that arises with Third World immigration is the dismal treatment of females. They are often not encouraged to become educated, are enslaved to husbands or families, and are otherwise prevented from assimilating. Attempts to Canadianize them often end in violence or banishment. Attempts to mix with other ethnic groups or races are met with intolerance by these families. Female genital mutilation is practiced by certain Arab and African immigrants, and charges have already been laid against a few sets of parents in Ontario. And one gynecologist told me that half of the abortions he performed were for East Indian or Chinese couples who did not want daughters, only sons.

Professor Borjas pointed out another difference between the immigration waves. Nearly one-third of the immigrants in the early 1900s who arrived went home because they couldn't cut it. In the 1980s, 22 percent left. But recent studies show that foreign-borns on welfare are less likely to leave the country the longer they are on assistance, compared to those who have never been on welfare.

"The magnetic effects of welfare raise fundamental questions about both the political legitimacy and economic viability of the welfare state," said Professor Borjas. Who is entitled to the safety net that American taxpayers pay for? And can the United States afford to extend that safety net to the rest of the world?" "Second, the empirical link between immigration and welfare is indisputable."

Like Canada, U.S. immigration participation in welfare began to rise after 1961 when Third World immigrants, mostly from Mexico and Asia, were allowed entry. In 1970, immigrants in the U.S. were less likely to receive assistance than native-borns. By 1980, according to the U.S. Census, immigrants were 1 percent more likely to receive help. By 1990, immigrants received a disproportionately larger share of the welfare benefits distributed. By 1998, 10 percent of immigrant households, and only 7 percent of native-born households, were on welfare. And the longer they were in the country, the more likely it was that immigrants would use the welfare system. Refugees from certain countries were the worst. For instance, 50 percent of all immigrants from Laos or Cambodia and 33 percent from the Soviet Union, Cuba, or Vietnam were on welfare.

The Business Immigrant Boondoggle

In 1986, the Mulroney government also initiated investor and entrepreneur immigration "fast track" schemes to attract well-heeled foreigners to the country as a means of creating jobs and economic activity. The rules were that those applying under the entrepreneur category had to employ five Canadians in a business and manage it personally. Those applying under the investor category had to put up at least $250,000 in British Columbia,

Ontario, and Quebec and only $150,000 elsewhere. In 1994, the thresholds were raised to $450,000. The investment was secured for three years in return for visas for the investor, spouse, and minor children. After fulfilling the residency requirement, the family could then apply to become Canadian citizens.

By 1995, consultants had found a loophole: investor-immigrants need only put up a down payment as part of their investment and they could borrow the rest. This meant that if someone heading a family of five put $100,000 down and borrowed $350,000 to become a landed immigrant, and eventually a citizen, the price of citizenship was a mere $20,000 per person. Considering the entitlements they would be given, in terms of social services and an ability to sponsor relatives, this was the windfall of a lifetime, hugely subsidized by Canadian taxpayers.

Worse than that was another loophole discovered by tax lawyers. The money could be put in an offshore trust in the Caribbean and could still meet the criteria as long as it was invested in Canadian securities. The investor did not have to pay Canadian income taxes on the income for five years, at which point he or she had to repatriate the funds and pay taxes on whatever capital gains were made. The argument in favor of this was that no investor would put his capital into a high-tax country like Canada without some kind of benefit.

The Americans, by contrast, imposed a dramatically higher threshold for entry to investors. "Business" immigrants had to invest US$1 million in the United States, had to pay taxes on that plus any other income the investor had around the world, and had to create jobs for Americans. Investors also were not guaranteed Green Cards, nor were they guaranteed citizenship. Both could take years to acquire.

Even though Canada's citizenship was a giveaway by comparison, the theory of attracting wealthy immigrants was sound in terms of economic policy. But, like other recent immigration initiatives, the bureaucracy proved totally incompetent in terms of design, implementation, or policing. For instance, I came across a case in 1986 that revealed the naïveté and/or negligence of immigration officials when I was a reporter at *The Toronto Star* and specialized in investigations into bad business practices. The gentleman calling me had a scam to report. He was a Canadian who did not want his name used because he had profited from the scam several times. But his conscience had bothered him, and he had stopped participating. His desire was to stop the culprit, an immigration lawyer.

He had been approached by the lawyer, from a prominent Bay Street firm, to sell his small chemical repackaging business. Located in Scarborough, it employed roughly 20 people and had revenues of several million dollars a year. He told the lawyer that his company was not for sale. The lawyer said that was okay and explained what would happen. He represented well-heeled Hong Kong clients who were desperately seeking to get a Canadian passport in a hurry, as the deadline loomed in 1997, for the handover of Hong Kong to mainland China. The easiest way to get in quickly was to apply as an investor-immigrant or entrepreneur-immigrant.

"The lawyer said 'what you do is sit down with me for an hour, sell your business on paper to me for X dollars to a Hong Kong investor and he will have signed a paper, which I will give to you simultaneously, agreeing to sell you back your business for X dollars minus $50,000,' he explained. "We can do six or seven of these transactions in an hour, with different investors. Each time you will make $50,000 profit, which means you can make yourself $300,000 or $350,000 without doing anything."

The man had sold, and repurchased, his business in this way several times. But it was clearly fraud designed to show immigration officials that these individuals had "invested" in Canada, employing 20 persons, when they actually had not. The lawyer explained that the department was "stupid" because all they wanted to know from investor-immigrant applicants was what investment they had made, for how much, and in what company. They never asked if they still owned it.

It was a cute trick, but not nearly as cute as another I came across in 1989 after I wrote my book, *Contrepreneurs*, about boiler rooms in

Amsterdam that defrauded investors of billions by selling phony Canadian stocks. These same fraudsters were eventually shut down by Dutch police and that, along with a stock market recession that began that year, put them out of the stock-peddling business. So they decided to flog Canadian citizenships around the world.

They began to use their stock peddling newsletters, sent to their lists of "suckers," to advertise citizenships for sale. One stock market tout sheet I obtained, which was mailed out by a ring of convicted Canadian fraudsters, promised citizenship for $250,000 without so much as a residency requirement. When I called the phone number listed for further information, the scam was explained in detail.

The person on the other end of the line promised that anyone, including fugitives or those with criminal records, could get into Canada if they invested $250,000 in Canadian securities. (They would of course help pick out those securities.) He said their consultancy firm would do the paperwork and organize entry for an additional fee of $50,000. The residency requirement was easy to get around, he explained. He said that an interested party could buy a condo or modest home, or rent one, then obtain a driver's licence and a car. This meant the investor-immigrant appeared to be living in Canada but would not have to. They could come and go as they pleased, by crossing first into the U.S., before taking a plane elsewhere. By doing so, their absences would go undetected because border crossings into the U.S. were unrecorded, so Canadian officials would have no way of finding out if the immigrant was in residency. Unfortunately, such residency fraud was easy.

Depressingly, I discovered in 1990 that one of the ringleaders of this group peddling citizenships had been granted investor-immigrant status in Vancouver within weeks of applying, and citizenship weeks later. I tipped off immigration and police officials about this, but nothing ever happened. Obviously, there was bribery involved, and his entry into Canada, despite a current criminal investigation underway into his activities as well as a criminal record, was evidently purchased from corrupt Canadian immigration officials.

Another immigrant-investor rip-off was explained to me in an interview in 1999 with offshore tax advisor Peter Sabourin, concerning the five-year, tax-free trust fund ride. These funds—which could be, and often were, more than the $250,000 or $450,000 minimum required—were placed into an immigration trust, which held the assets. After the five years was up, the assets became taxable along with any worldwide income these people had. Canada's rules stipulate that if you have foreign property worth more than $100,000, you must report that plus any assets or trusts you control.

"But a wealthy Asian would bring $1 million, put it into an immigrant trust for the five years, but keep his other $60 million back home in Korea, or Hong Kong, or Taiwan, or wherever, and not report its income," said Mr. Sabourin.

He estimates that only 4 percent of total assets abroad are declared by investor immigrants in Canada.

"What happens is they are supposed to declare worldwide income after the five years, but they get out of it by loaning or gifting their $60 million offshore assets to their mom or whatever," he said. "This is a trick. Or they give her a demand loan of $60 million without interest required, so it means they still control these assets but don't declare that to Revenue Canada. It's a racket, and these immigrants are killing us."

In another scam, he said the immigrant brings in $1 million, buys a hotel here, borrows his own money from his mother to buy it, pays interest to his "mom" on the borrowings to buy the hotel, and the interest is exactly the income the hotel generates. So a cheque is written offshore to his "mom," which is deducted as an expense from his income, meaning the hotel business never pays taxes. That's "legal laundering," or evasion, he said.

Another scheme is known as the "the Persian carpet" and is a favorite evasion technique perpetrated by Middle East investor-immigrants. They pay an inflated price for carpets from an accomplice, or from themselves indirectly, import them as a business, go bankrupt, sell the carpets in bankruptcy at a loss, and write off the "losses" from the artificially inflated price paid against other income.

"Hotels are popular for Asian investor immigrants," said Mr. Sabourin. "They buy a $5 million hotel to meet the investor criteria. They lease it to a B.C. holding company. The next immigrant-investor comes in and buys a new class of shares issued in that same hotel. Another one comes in, and another, and so on. You could end up with 20 people declaring that they own the same hotel."

Another hotel scam he described involved the construction of a hotel for, say $20 million. Individual rooms were leased out for a fee so that lessees could claim they were investing in Canada in order to meet the requirements. Once accepted as an investor-immigrant, they could then sublet the rooms back to the hotel owner at a loss and write that off their income taxes.

"It goes on and on," he said. "There are many variations, and nobody's playing by the rules. The Americans have investor-immigrant programs, but they are much tougher and have better laws and fewer loopholes."

Solutions should be simple, he added. "These demand loans should have set interest rates and the Canadian relative who loaned the money should be taxed on the interest rate charged. The repayment of principal should be limited in terms of years," he said.

In 1990, just four years after the implementation of these two business categories, Ottawa's auditor general documented the department's negligence. "During the first nine months of 1989, 2,345 entrepreneurs became permanent residents. Our audit revealed that only 60 percent of these entrepreneurs were landed with terms and conditions imposed. Less than half of those were required to report to Immigration Canada to provide evidence of compliance with conditions imposed. Until the fall of 1989 there were no entrepreneurs referred to inquiry for breach of conditions."

The most notorious example of an entrepreneur-immigrant involved Lee Chau-Ping, her estranged husband, and two sons, who fled with her in

1992 in order to escape arrest and extradition to mainland China for drug trafficking. She told Canadian immigration officials that she owned a restaurant in Canton and had $1.1 million in assets. Then she pledged to buy a Chicken Delight franchise in Saskatchewan. She also bought two homes, two cars, and other assets in Vancouver. Hong Kong police later found out she never owned a restaurant in China and never bought one in Saskatchewan.

In 1999, another glimpse into the mess occurred when an official with Citizenship and Immigration in charge of Maritime investor-immigrants wrote a memo that became public about the amount of fraud and misrepresentation involved. He estimated that, of the 20,000 entering Canada under the program, many were scam artists.

"This program assists and promotes citizenship-of-convenience fraud, promotes abuse in national and provincial social programs and, in my opinion, is a national disgrace," wrote the official, Paul Coolen of Halifax. His memo was obtained by newspapers under access to information legislation. Another internal Immigration Department study in the mid-1990s showed that 80 percent of so-called "entrepreneur-immigrants" who promise to create jobs had not fulfilled their end of the bargain.

In 1999, another scandal broke.

"David Webber is a senior forensic accountant with the World Bank in Washington D.C. Between 1994 and 1998 he was engaged by the Department of Immigration to conduct compliance reviews of 42 immigrant investor funds. Coincident with this, three other accountants were engaged to review 60 additional funds," wrote former vice-chairman of the Immigration Appeal Board Charles Campbell in his book *Betrayal and Deceit*. "Mr. Webber described those immigrant-investor programs, designed as they were to provide foreign investment for small businesses in Canada, as being riddled with fraud. He said claims made by Immigrant Canada about the program's success were a gross exaggeration and that rules introduced by Ottawa to combat that fraud in 1999 are completely ineffective."

One example involved investment by an immigrant fund in a theater project in Atlantic Canada for $750,000 that simply did not exist. "A lot of people made a lot of money, mostly lawyers and consultants who set up these bogus investments," said Webber. "The middlemen made hundreds of millions of dollars," and he rejected claims by Ottawa spokesmen that the schemes had brought $4.5 billion worth of investments into the country. After rules in most provinces tightened up investor-immigrant fund practices, Quebec continued with the same rules.

In his Senate testimony in 2001, Martin Collacott criticized these categories of "business" immigrants.

"There have been some major problems with that program. It was suggested 10 years ago in major reports that we may not even need the program because it is supposed to go into risk capital, and there is enough risk capital in Canada. It has been very popular for immigration consultants. Basically, you can immigrate to Canada without meeting normal immigrant requirements through this program. The average person coming in has relatively little education and cannot speak English or French. It is tremendously popular in certain circles. It has been complicated because of special provisions for Quebec to some extent. However, long ago it was suggested that it was not really required in terms of Canadian needs."

James Bissett, also a former Immigration official, added in his testimony: "It is a program that is vulnerable to a lot of abuse. We know that has happened in the past. I am inclined to agree with Mr. Collacott that we really do not need it. If immigrants with a lot of money want to come to Canada and to invest their money here, they are free to come. They do not need to come through this program. The program can and has been used by the Russian Mafia, by the Chinese triads, and others to buy their way into Canada."

William Bauer added, "I would agree with what has been said. It is a shadowy area, as you know. It is hard to pin it down. Even when people are prosecuted, as they are about once every three years, not too many facts come out. I agree with the others, it is an unnecessary program. When you think of the chaps who were involved on September 11, they have got lots of money available to them. It is a wonderful way to plant sleepers in your society for the time when you push the button. It may be five years from now, but it sort of avoids difficulties about security or anything else."

Canada's business immigration strategy has been an unmitigated disaster and is slowly being phased out. At fault was, once again, an incompetent bureaucracy that failed to research applicants properly and then failed to police them. Immigration funds sprung up across the country, often run by unscrupulous people, and an estimated $1.2 billion of investor money disappeared in scams. All but those operated out of Quebec, where regulators were more proficient, were shut down by the federal government in the mid-1990s after scandals.

"There was a systemic weakness, and the whole entrepreneur category was a scam," said immigration consultant Richard Kurland. "It's been all cleaned up now [2002]. It didn't work any better in the U.S., where the category is still on the books but is not used. It's a rich man's visa, and who wants that? Besides, you have to be concerned about people coming in this way because it's been so easy to get in the usual way."

Immigration consultant David Lesperance, of Global Relocation Consultants, disagreed that it had been cleaned up and said in testimony in 2001 that it was easy to cheat and get citizenship as an "investor" immigrant without living or working in Canada. The wealthy use this category to bypass immigration and "buy" passports for their families. They immigrate under the investor program, move their families here to get our education and health care, do not file tax returns, spend little time here, and make no contribution to Canada. After three years they can apply for and get citizenship. "Abusers are easily skirting the entire regime," he said.

In his submission, called "A Scoundrel's Guide," he revealed how to easily circumvent the law and procedures, and obtain citizenship without paying taxes and without spending time in Canada.

"The key is to maintain a low profile from both port of entry immigration officers and Revenue Canada, while ultimately being in a position to satisfy citizenship officials in three years that you have been physically present in Canada for all of the past three years.

"Therefore a scoundrel should:

1. Take all steps to avoid Revenue Canada knowing that you exist. This would include:

   a) NOT applying for a Social Insurance Number unless caught in a 'random citizenship audit'

   b) NOT filing a tax return in Canada;

   c) NOT holding any brokerage or bank accounts in your name so as to avoid the generation of T5 forms.

   d) NOT working for a Canadian employer so as to avoid the generation of a T4 form; and

   e) NOT applying for any government benefits. Note: If you really want to abuse the system, have your spouse and children apply for benefits but make sure that they have little to no taxable income or capital gains attributable to them.

2. Take all steps possible to avoid port of entry immigration officers from determining if you have been outside of Canada for more than 183 days in the past year. This would include: not applying for a Returning Resident Permit; limiting the number of entries you make into Canada; and entering at a port of entry where there is a lower level of examination and little to no chance of the entry being recorded. For example, do

not take an international flight from Hong Kong to Vancouver. Fly from Hong to Chicago and buy a pair of Chicago Cubs tickets. Then take a flight to North Dakota and have someone drive a car from Winnipeg to meet you. When you cross present a Manitoba driver's licence claiming you went to Chicago to see a baseball game. Make sure you leave your passport and overseas plane tickets in your safety deposit box in Chicago. Make sure you have your Permanent Resident visa paper in your overnight bag along with some Canadian business cards and a doctored appointment calendar showing Canadian appointments. When completing your citizenship application form (CIT0002) indicate that you have not left Canada during the past three years."

He said the problem was that citizenship applications do not require filed tax returns or a copy of the applicant's passport. In other words, we are letting people into the country in the hopes that they will live here and make an economic contribution without asking for evidence that they have done either before granting them the privilege of citizenship.

Failing to Help Real Refugees

What refugees? Canada is so busy accommodating bogus refugee claimants that it has not done its fair share of helping real refugees, or people who have been uprooted permanently and are camping in tents in faraway places.

For instance, refugee claimants Lai Changxing and his wife, Tsang Mingna, were accused in 2000 of running the biggest corruption and smuggling ring to hit China since Communist rule began in 1949. They fled to Canada by using fake Hong Kong passports, and were arrested in an Ontario casino, where he allegedly had gambled away $500,000 in a summer.

China sought his extradition, but his refugee claim is that he should be allowed to remain in Canada because the *Charter of Rights* protects him from China's death penalty. Lai and his wife were jailed, due to the extradition, but were able to convince immigration authorities to let them live, in luxury, under house arrest. The family, including his wife and two children, moved into their Vancouver condo, where Mr. Lai agreed to pay $80,000 a month to live under the guard of a private security firm. Another fugitive-refugee in Vancouver, Thai banker Rakesh Saxena, was also in jail awaiting extradition, but moved into his fancy waterfront condo on False Creek at a cost of $40,000 a month for his security guards. The arrangements were approved by a B.C. court and upheld on appeal. Lawyers for both men represented the arrangements as a cost saving to Canadian taxpayers. Mr. Lai's refugee claim was rejected in June 2002, but he said he will exhaust all appeal procedures.

Despite a proliferation of such "champagne" refugees, the United Nations High Commissioner for Refugees, Ruud Lubbers, patted the Liberal government on the back in 2002 over its enlightened refugee policy. But the truth is we don't know how many of the 472,857 alleged refugees allowed into Canada between 1986 and 2000 were actually "real" refugees according to the United Nation's own convention definition.

That is because Canada's refugee policy is out of control. At the same time, its indiscriminate nature has crowded out entry to the country of real refugees, according to James Bissett. He said in his testimony, before the Senate in 2001, that Canada was contributing nearly $25 million a year to the United Nations High Commissioner on Refugees—only about $1 per refugee—while spending billions on "alleged" refugees here at home.

"I've seen many camps with poor people who don't have money to buy food; many are sick and most are women and children," he said. In contrast, it costs $150 million for the Immigration and Refugee Board to process some 30,000 to 40,000 refugee applications a year. "The main beneficiaries are young men, mostly 18 to 25 years old. They're street-smart and smart enough to buy their way in. We're spending all our money on them. It's a charade designed to make lawyers rich and serve as a moral salve for the conscience of ordinary Canadians, and does little to help refugees in camps."

In fact, he says "refugees" is a misnomer. "They are people coming here claiming to be refugees. We do not know anything about them," he told the senators. "None of them is screened for security. None of them is screened for health or criminality."

Many of Canada's refugee claimants are far from being ragtag displaced persons carrying all their possessions in the world in a sack. They arrive first class on flights from Hong Kong or Frankfurt wearing suits and carrying fancy luggage. They are met by drivers with cars and have cell phones and phone numbers of oncologists, or drug dealers, or tennis clubs to join. Once they arrive at a Canadian airport they make a refugee claim, and then up to 10 years of legal games begin.

Sometimes, they go to the United States first and drive in, or catch a flight out of Kennedy or O'Hare to Toronto. They claim they have no documents even though they could not have boarded their planes without any proof of citizenship or identification papers. Everything's disappeared.

There are also refugee claimants who have no intention of living in Canada. They are students in the U.S. who have found a way to make money to support themselves.

"Pakistani land border claimants commonly claim that agents took their passports from them after arriving at Kennedy airport," said a confidential government report. "It is common knowledge that public funds from claims in Canada will support the [claimant's] continuing studies in the U.S."

They make their claim to get welfare payments in Canada. To do so is quite simple. They make a claim, request welfare, and furnish a maildrop address (usually an accomplice's) who mails on the cheques. They may or may not come back for a hearing, which could take months to arrange, after several postponements on the part of the claimant. If they don't show, a deportation order may take months or years more to issue, by which time they, and their accomplice at that address, have disappeared. Any warrant for the deportee is useless because the person has disappeared, or used an alias, or gone to the U.S. where law enforcement officials cannot legally enforce a Canadian deportation order.

Welfare scams perpetrated by foreign students studying at U.S. universities may be one explanation as to why an average of 20 percent of refugee claimants never show up for hearings and simply disappear. These foreign students show up at the border without identification. After a brief interview, they get their refugee-claim papers and proceed to the nearest welfare office. Investigators told newspapers in November 2001 that this fraud is organized, and students are given a Canadian address where welfare cheques are sent, cashed with a portion kept by organizers, and then forwarded electronically into bank accounts south of the border or anywhere else in the world. Ontario at least requires welfare recipients to work or attend school. But the schools never take attendance, so fraudsters sign up for Learnfare and skip classes.

In fall 2001, there was an incident at the Niagara Falls border crossing. Sudanese students attending the University of Tennessee were dropped off at the border and the car was searched by customs. The two students were returned to the U.S. after attempting to claim refugee status. Fortunately, their passports were found in the car. The driver confessed. After being caught, the two students said it was common knowledge among foreign students that Canada was an easy mark.

Another "big racket," Mr. Bissett told the Senate, involves groups of Argentines who travel to the U.S. because they don't need a visa. They then present themselves to Canada as refugees, are put up in hotels, and dine on welfare money. After they finish their two- or three-month Canadian holiday, he said, many simply return home. A percentage of Mexican refugee claimants have started to do the same thing. "I'm told that motels in southwestern Ontario are full of refugee claimants while Canadians pay their bills."

Mr. Bissett believes that refugees caught with false identification should be detained "until we know who they are," and that criminal activity should bring swift consequences: "If you're a newcomer to the country and you get into trouble with the law, you should be sent home. That's a given."

The fastest way to stop the flood is for Canada to adopt the "safe third country" rule. Most refugee claimants come through the U.S. Some 12,000 each year stream in from the United States through southwestern Ontario border points. Latin Americans are funneled, and counseled, by an organization in Buffalo called Vive La Casa, and Arabs are funneled, and counseled, by an organization in Detroit called Freedom House.

"The costs of our asylum system are enormous. This year, the operating costs for processing refugee claimants will be close to $150 million. This doesn't take into account the much higher costs for providing social assistance, housing, legal, and medical services—all at taxpayers' expense. The Refugee Board is composed of about 180 members, all political appointees. Most have had no experience in refugee matters," said Mr. Bissett. In 1997, a consultative group of experts recommended that Ottawa scrap the Refugee Board and employ career officers specialized in refugee matters. Ottawa rejected this in favor of the current patronage system.

"Canada has not implemented reforms because of pressure from immigration lawyers and other special-interest groups. And so, as other countries tighten their rules, we receive more asylum-seekers. And our new bill [passed in December 2001] proposes to broaden the UN definition of 'refugee' by establishing a new 'protected person' class [those claiming that they would be subjected to cruel and unusual punishment if they were returned]. The bill incorporates into legislation the somewhat vague UN Convention against Torture, and it guarantees a 'fair hearing' to anyone who claims to be persecuted [which seems to preclude prescreening of claimants, as is done by other countries]," added Mr. Bissett.

"The current legislation allows the immigration minister to prevent a war criminal, terrorist, or serious criminal from making a refugee claim. The new bill demands that an ineligibility ruling in these suspected categories must be done within 72 hours or the individual will be eligible to make a claim," he said.

"This is a joke. It is almost impossible to complete security and criminal checks in 72 hours; most of these cases will then proceed to the Immigration and Refugee Board and become entangled in the inevitable delays and legal proceedings. If we are dealing with terrorists and criminals, this is a big step backward. *Bill C-11* is a disaster. It plays into the hands of professional smugglers. It leaves Canada wide open for easy entry to undesirables. It seems designed to ensure that the bad guys can never be sent home. Does anyone still wonder why our allies doubt Canada's seriousness in the fight against terrorism?" said Mr. Bissett.

The highest ranking former immigration official to publicly criticize the system at the Senate hearings has been Jack Manion, former immigration deputy minister.

"The refugee process has become so mammoth that it is soaking up virtually all the available resources in the immigration portfolio," said Mr. Manion. "Governments in Canada are now spending something in the order of $4 billion on immigration and refugee matters. Most of that is spent unproductively. There is not enough money for enforcement. There is not enough money for visa control overseas and proper co-ordination. Proceedings are started and then run automatically over the telephone and by paper. It is no way to run an immigration program. I am horrified by what I see and what I hear every day from friends of mine who have connections in the immigration service. The morale in the immigration service is deplorable."

"It's a disgrace when people like me write letters successively to one minister after another and get pre-printed replies from correspondence clerks," he told the senators. "They should listen to people other than the interest groups, if they want to find out what Canada thinks and what can be done about these problems."

Another problem with the refugee determination process is that claimants can lie without any consequences. There is no cross-examination, no ability to call witnesses to refute testimony, and no penalties for perjury, even if discovered.

"There is a very basic flaw in the system," former immigration member William Bauer testified. "The law holds that unless the trier of the claim has very strong evidence of internal contradictions, one must accept all testimony given under oath as true. No other witnesses can be called, and there are no penalties for perjury. I recall one occasion when a Sri Lankan Tamil claimant submitted a claim that was identical to the last detail to one submitted by another Tamil whose hearing was scheduled later in the day. They were represented by the same lawyer, who showed no embarrassment at all when the coincidence was drawn to his attention."

In 2001, an open letter was published in newspapers and signed by Mr. Collacott, former ambassador to several countries; Mr. Manion; Charles Campbell, formerly vice-chair of the Immigration Appeal Board; J. C. Best, former assistant deputy minister of immigration and Canadian high commissioner; and Des Verma, former member of the Immigration and Refugee Board.

"Our refugee program is facing widespread abuse. Canadians are proud of their tradition of accepting refugees fleeing persecution," said their open letter published in several newspapers. "But a particularly serious problem arising from the refugee determination system is the lack of control over our borders resulting from the application of the 50-year-old United Nations Convention on the Status of Refugees and from an interpretation of the *Charter of Rights*. Our adherence to the Convention makes it possible for virtually anyone who sets foot on our soil or arrives at our borders to enter our refugee determination system and stand a good chance of never being forced to leave.

"Our system, arguably the most generous in the world, has thus become a magnet not only for tens of thousands of persons who are simply seeking better economic opportunities but also for criminals and terrorists who are fugitives from justice in their own countries. Because *Charter* protection is now available to everyone on our territory, it is also now almost impossible to remove serious criminals and terrorists, along with many others who should not be allowed to remain here."

"Our first responsibility is to Canadians. When the *Charter of Rights and Freedoms* was being drafted, those preparing it were warned that, if its wording did not restrict its application to Canadians, it could be used to bypass and frustrate our immigration laws. This is precisely what has happened.

"The result is a 1985 Supreme Court decision that concluded that the *Charter* applied to anyone on Canadian soil or within Canada's territorial waters, whether here legally or not. In consequence, we have the most time-consuming and expensive refugee determination system in the world.

"In the circumstances, the application of the *Charter* to those who have no right of residency here needs to be re-examined as a matter of urgency. The relevant sections should henceforth apply only to Canadian citizens and legal permanent residents of Canada. This could be achieved by amending the *Charter* or invoking the notwithstanding clause.

"There is a proposal in *Bill C-11* [passed December 2001] to extend *Charter* rights to anyone in the world who wants to come to Canada. This will make the situation significantly worse than it already is. While it may be a boon to immigration lawyers, it will throw into even greater disarray the efficient and effective management of our immigration program and the protection of our national sovereignty. The government, regrettably, has shown no disposition to re-examine this important and sensitive issue in spite of the extremely negative impact it is having on Canada."

They concluded: "We must emphasize that Parliament's will—as expressed in the Immigration Act prior to the 1985 court decision—was that there should be no right of appeal against a decision to deny a Canadian visa, except in the case of applications for the immediate families of legal Canadian residents. This corresponds with the laws of most other countries of the world. For Canada to throw away this provision seriously undermines our sovereignty."

Success or Failure?

The only way to evaluate any public policy is to examine its objectives and whether these are being met or not. When immigration sticks to economics, it works beautifully. But when social engineering gets involved, problems occur. For instance, Ontario wanted to restock Ontario with Britons after the Second World War. Then the federal government, under Pierre Trudeau, wanted to do the opposite. Trudeau eliminated the privileges that British immigrants enjoyed over others and then heavily promoted multiculturalism throughout English Canada.

Another political objective was to encourage immigrants to settle in Quebec in order to frustrate attempts by French zealots to secede. In reaction, Quebec responded by taking over immigration operations in its region in the hopes of attracting francophone immigrants who would be sympathetic to secessionist aspirations. Quebec also extracted from Ottawa most of the immigrant and refugee settlement funds, despite the fact that it gets less than 20 percent of the flow.

But the most dramatic departure in terms of immigration policy has been the misguided demographic case and the controversial refugee determination situation. The removal of discretion at the border, as a result of the 1985 *Singh* Supreme Court decision, was followed by mass amnesty, along with the perpetuation of a patronage-driven bureaucracy.

Now Canada finds itself with an immigration/refugee set of policies that are at odds with public opinion because they no longer clearly deliver the traditional economic benefits. The problem is not immigration *per se*, but the failure to design and effectively implement goals. This has been due to a lack of resources, political stubbornness, political cynicism, incompetence, malfeasance, and an uncontrollable refugee determination system.

The Abdication of Protection

"The system is corrupt and the immigration board has become a wretched monster that's out of control," said Liberal David Anderson in 1992. He had been with the immigration board in previous years, and after the Liberal election in 1993 became a cabinet minister.

Asymmetrical Migration—In, Never Out

What criminal or terrorist problems do immigrants and refugees visit upon Canada? How many have we let in who should have been screened out? What proportion of crimes committed in Canada are by refugees or immigrants? Are they more likely to break the law than native-born Canadians? If so, which groups are most undesirable in terms of criminality? This information is unobtainable because it is unknown, uncollected, or is kept under lock and key. The last time a police official in Toronto released figures about crime by ethnic group, a furor erupted from special-interest groups, heads rolled, and promises were made by politicians to never allow that to happen again.

That's probably reasonable. And it's also reasonable to assume that there is not an immigration system anywhere in the world that would be able to completely block undesirables from entry. That would be impossible. But any system should be able to correct and to remove undesirables who slip through. Not Canada. There is no reasonable or efficient means of deporting people, no matter how serious their misdeeds.

This is unacceptable. After all, Canada has enough of its own home-grown criminals, fraudsters, and terrorists without importing more. Immigration and refugee status, even citizenship, are privileges, not rights, and serious crimes should result in automatic removal. Migration should not be a one-way street. Tough legislation that would immediately detain and deport wrongdoers, convicted of serious offences, is urgently needed. Such measures would not only act as a deterrent but also would rid our streets, alleyways, and jails of dangerous strangers. They would also eliminate the reason why many terrorists, undesirables, and criminals come here. Word is out that once you are allowed into Canada, you're never tossed out. In 2001, the government admitted there were 27,000 outstanding deportation orders that had not been executed.

The federal government has continuously failed to provide sufficient resources for enforcement or investigative purposes when it comes to immigrants and refugees. New laws passed since September 11 have bolstered the investigative and removal capabilities of suspected terrorists. But such measures, even if utilized, are sure to be eroded through court challenges. The 72-hour national security detention requirement is also impossible to meet, given current staffing constraints, according to the immigration department's union chief. So, as matters now stand, Canada has an asymmetrical immigration policy. We invite people in but have virtually no mechanism by which to remove them once they have arrived.

The Immigration and Refugee Board can order a landed immigrant, a landed refugee, or a refugee claimant deported. But there are a host of appeals possible. If ordered deported, and not in custody, the person is asked to voluntarily remove him- or herself. No one checks up on this, and many people disappear, go underground, or reapply under another name to start the process all over again.

Politicians are in major denial about this problem. But what follows is testimony by professionals about the deportation situation from the December 2001 Senate hearings.

Senator Di Nino: I understand we have some 27,000 people who have been ordered deported and are still hanging around the country. I wonder if either the RCMP or CSIS would like to make a comment on that. Why do we still have 27,000 people still in this country who have been ordered deported?

William Lenton, assistant commissioner, Royal Canadian Mounted Police: The way the system works is that once a person is ordered deported they have 30 days to leave the country. There is a requirement that if they do not leave the country, or have not signaled their departure within 30 days, then the warrant is generated and it goes on the system. Whether or not the people are still in Canada is a subject of debate. They may have left and just failed to declare their departure. They may have left within the 30 days. They may have stayed here for 45 days and then did not want to declare their departure because if they did they might face some kind of risk. I do not believe you can make the direct link that there are 27,000 on the system, therefore 27,000 are still within the confines of the boundaries of Canada. The CIC [Citizenship and Immigration Canada] tries to search out and identify the high risk elements of those. If there are ones that are of particular high risk, we will make a positive effort to find them and remove them. The other ones become a question of volume and a question of assets available to do that.

The Chairman: This is a simple layman's view of the world. You have an individual who has been told to leave the country. Presumably, at the time that he gets that information, the individual is either in custody or certainly in a place where people know his location because they need to deliver the message to him. I assume it is an administrative or judicial tribunal that has delivered that message, correct?

Mr. Lenton: Yes, it is the Immigration and Refugee Review Board that makes the determination.

The Chairman: Is there then a decision for that individual to leave the country because you regard him as a security risk?

Mr. Lenton: He may not necessarily be determined as a security risk. There is a determination that is made. That is a determination made by the review board.

The Chairman: I am not saying all 27,000 are security risks, I am saying some of them are security risks.

Mr. Lenton: Yes, sir.

The Chairman: However, regardless of the reason the decision is made that they must leave the country, they are allowed to go free. What is puzzling me, as a simple layman, is that if it is decided that an individual should leave the country because they are a security risk, why do we then get into a game of hide and seek? I do not understand why, for those cases that are security risks, they are not simply detained until they are required to leave the country. Mr. [Ward] Elcock [Director of the Canadian Security Intelligence Service or CSIS], do you wish to say something?

Mr. Elcock: There is a provision in the *Immigration Act* now, section 40.1, which allows the removal of people who are deemed a security risk. It has a wider application but has been used most often in the case of people who are considered to be a security risk. That provision provides for arrest and detention. A number of people are still detained in Canadian jails at this point. Prior to arrest, there can be detention for whatever period of time until the matter is dealt with, and ultimately for deportation from Canada. The only reason that in some cases people have not been deported in those instances have been because there is nowhere to send them; either the country is deemed unacceptable to send them back to because of the fear of torture or execution—and that is an issue that is now before the Supreme Court—or the countries are simply unwilling to accept them, period.

The Chairman: In a case like that, does the individual remain in jail?

Mr. Elcock: We have not actually had a case where anyone has not gone somewhere yet, but in theory that could happen. In other cases, for example, the refugee is someone who has been found not to be a refugee. For example, in the case of [Millennium Bomber] Ahmed Ressam, he was ordered deported from the country, but because the country to which he would have been deported was Algeria, and there was a decision that he could not be deported to Algeria, he was not deported there and he was allowed to go free. That was a decision taken at that point by the government.

The Chairman: Would that decision have been taken by the Immigration and Refugee Board or by the government?

Mr. Elcock: By the government.

The same day as that testimony occurred, so did disturbing remarks by Janina Lebon, national vice president, Canada Employment and Immigration Union, about the staff available to do removals or enforcement of any kind.

"With respect to section 100 of *Bill C-11*, the claims [involving suspected national security risks] are to be processed within a 72-hour time frame. This process involves personal interviews, basically a resumption of what we used to do 10 years ago when we had face-to-face interviews, spoke to our clients, talked to them and got our information. We currently use the mail-in process. Now, it is also expected that all the necessary background and medical checks will be initiated. There is no way for the RCMP to do a complete criminal background check, for CSIS to do a security check, or for the medical services to complete any of their checks in the 72-hour frame. Therefore, we will not be able to confirm the identity of undocumented claimants, and we will not know the state of the health of some claimants. If you recall, Fort Erie last year had the multiple resistant tuberculosis concern, so there are problems with infectious diseases.

"As to whether we have sufficient resources to carry out the requirements of section 100, while we have the 72-hour deadline, who will be doing what we call the regular immigration work, the work of doing the landings, the student unemployment authorization and the reports on criminality and other inadmissible clients? Who will determine the priority? Those are major issues. Furthermore, who will deal with the thousands of files in backlog?

"The biggest issue, particularly for my office, will be the pre-removal risk assessment …. This means that all persons who have an effective removal order are eligible for a pre-removal risk assessment. No one can be removed from Canada until that risk assessment is done. This assessment is not limited to refugee claimants only. It includes everyone. If one looks at the act it says, "you may file a request for this assessment." That means no one is really excluded. If I am not mistaken, there are some 27,000 files—which is the rumored number—of removal cases right now. They will all need to be reviewed.

"I will give you the example I have used. A student has overstayed. A departure order has been issued against him or her. This student is entitled to a review. The problem is it must be recently done, and the figure I have heard is that it must be done within 30 days. Therefore, the assessment is done and it is negative, but the person concerned is not removed because they have disappeared and we cannot find them. Then they re-appear six months later. A new pre-removal risk assessment must be done. This is an area where we will have problems with resources, but the bigger issue is how many removals will we be doing effectively? I would say we are looking at a trickle of removals to be done. That is of a major concern because we want to remove people who are supposed to be removed as quickly as possible. This, in effect, will not happen with this new process.

"My last major area that I will cover is the area of resources. The department must address the issue of adequate resources so we can carry out our duties under this act. Unlike most departments, Immigration underwent two rounds of downsizing. We were downsized first in 1993, and then a second time in 1995 and 1996. Our figures were reduced by almost half. We are at approximately 4,000 currently. When I started, we were well over 7,000. I was one of the people who got downsized in 1993 and I am now in what is known as the Greater Toronto Enforcement Office. Retirements are further reducing the ranks of our experienced, qualified staff. The recruitment of new staff is slow. The retention of some of these people is also problematic because they feel they are not being properly compensated so they leave. We have had a number who have left, including brand-new post-secondary recruitments who were with us six months and then went off to what they feel are better jobs.

"The issue of training for both the new staff, and ongoing training for current staff, is of a major concern, particularly as we will be going into a new act. What are the provisions that the department has put in for this new training? One of the issues for the inland officers, as well as enforcement, is that they must write nearly perfect reports because those reports are challenged and scrutinized in the courts, and we have many that end up in the courts. There is an issue here of proper legal documents. The accommodation issues, such as physical layout, where we keep our refugees during the 72 hours, all must be addressed prior to implementation. These are just some of the remarks I feel are necessary to make."

Removing war criminals, terrorists, or torturers who have become citizens is difficult, even under the new *Immigration Act*, according to David Matas, a refugee lawyer who made a presentation to the Senate on behalf of B'nai B'rith Canada.

"The first problem I have with the bill is that it does not have clear rules about who is removable. It sets up a system of discretion such that some people, who are in the category of terrorist, torturers, war criminals, and criminals against humanity, can be allowed to stay at the discretion of the minister, and there is a discretionary section," he said. "We also need to integrate citizenship and immigration with criminal proceedings so that if someone is convicted of a war crime, crime against humanity, torture, or terrorism, that should be enough for revocation of citizenship and deportation, which is not the case now."

The Refugee from Hell

The worst example of immigration incompetence—from screening and processing to enforcement—involved a Canadian resident, who came into the country as a refugee claimant, working for Osama bin Laden's al-Qaeda in Montreal. He, and other members of a Montreal cell, intended to blow up the Los Angeles International Airport, where 186,000 passengers travel every day. Fortunately, the ringleader was caught at the border. Ahmed Ressam was arrested December 14, 1999 in Port Angeles, Washington, when he panicked after questioning by a U.S. border agent. He bolted, only to be tackled by officers at a nearby intersection. A search of his car turned up 12 plastic bags in the wheel wells, containing 60 kilograms of explosives, including RDX and nitroglycerin, four boxes containing electrical panels connected to a Casio watch, and a nine-volt battery. During subsequent searches, RCMP officers found a map in Ressam's apartment showing three southern California airports circled in pen, among them the Los Angeles International Airport. The Ressam case exposed gaping holes in Canada's refugee determination system—holes that still have not been repaired.

In April 2001, he was convicted of plotting to blow up the Los Angeles International Airport. Weeks later, he began cooperating with authorities to reduce his jail time by fingering accomplices. His story is not unique and illustrates how easily Osama bin Laden's organization and other Arab terrorist groups established strategic beachheads in Canada.

On September 23, 1997, I wrote a news story in the *Financial Post* that exposed the existence of at least two dozen Algerian terrorists in Montreal. "These are very dangerous people and they have been hiding in Montreal for some months," said a French police source I quoted.

One of these "very dangerous" terrorists was Ahmed Ressam.

He arrived by plane at Mirabel Airport in February 1994 and sought refugee status immediately. A statement was taken the night of his arrival by a refugee officer. Mr. Ressam signed it. It was supposed to give his history and the reasons why he sought refuge. As court documents later showed in his bombing trial, Mr. Ressam did not disclose in his statement that he was a member of Algeria's militant Armed Islamic Group (AIG), one of the most dangerous terrorist groups in the world.

However, he did say he was a suspected Islamic terrorist and had spent 15 months in an Algerian prison for arms dealing. He claimed that he then fled to Morocco, Spain, and France, where he obtained a false French passport and a passenger ticket to Canada. French speaking, he headed for Montreal.

Despite his admission of holding a fake French passport and his admission of being a criminal and a possible extremist, immigration staff at the airport could merely take his statement, take his fingerprints, and let him go. Like other refugees, Mr. Ressam was automatically entitled to welfare, health care, legal aid, and a Social Insurance Number so he could find employment. He went on welfare immediately and moved into a "safe house" with other Algerian terrorists.

Evidence later supplied by French authorities showed that Mr. Ressam lied in his refugee claim statement. He was actually in France in 1993, at the time he claims to have been imprisoned and tortured in an Algerian prison. So he did not need protection because he was already in a safe country,

France. Under the United Nations convention, he could have been sent back to France. He wasn't.

Mr. Ressam was required, as are all refugee claimants, to show up at a hearing to determine whether he could stay permanently in Canada as a refugee. He never showed up for his hearing.

Police in several countries believe that Mr. Ressam was part of a cell linked to Osama bin Laden and al-Qaeda. The terrorists operated out of Mr. Ressam's apartment, supplying legal advice, black market passports, and money to Islamic militants who were involved in terrorist attacks in France and Turkey. Telephone, mail, and money transfer records link the apartment's tenants to extremists in Western Europe, the Balkans, and Asia.

While they were busy with such activities, these men, and others like them, rejected legitimate employment. Instead, they supplemented their welfare payments with the proceeds of crime. Within months of arriving, Mr. Ressam and his roommate were arrested by Montreal police for pickpocketing elderly women at a Sears store. Even though both men were refugees, or guests, in Canada who had failed to show up for their refugee hearings, they were not detained, nor did immigration officials attempt to deport them. Months later, Mr. Ressam was arrested a second time in Vancouver for stealing luggage at its airport.

Mr. Ressam should have been deported from Canada within months of his arrival. But he simply ignored, or his lawyer maneuvered around, rulings. In 1995, the Immigration and Refugee Board decided that Mr. Ressam had abandoned his refugee claim because he failed to show up for his hearing the year before. To avoid deportation, he appealed this decision to the Federal Court of Canada, with a lawyer paid for by Canadian taxpayers, and lost his challenge in 1996. He still was not ordered deported, even after losing his appeal because, at the time, Canada had stopped deportations to Algeria due to the civil war underway there.

Instead of detaining or jailing him, the immigration department simply let him loose on the condition that he would report regularly to an immigration officer. He eventually stopped showing up, and there was no real effort to track him down. Finally, on May 4, 1998, some four years after entering Canada, Mr. Ressam's name appeared on an arrest warrant for deportation. It was entered into the national police database a month later. But that did not matter. By that time, he had already created a false identity and was easily able to obtain a valid, *not counterfeit*, Canadian passport in a fake name. He chose a French Canadian–sounding alias, Benni Antoine Norris and furnished two fake pieces of identification, a Quebec baptismal certificate containing the forged signature of a Catholic priest, and a fake Université de Montréal student card. He attached his photograph.

The passport application form and the fake documents were delivered to the Canadian Passport Office in a Montreal suburb by a small-time criminal named Bert Eugene, an immigrant from Haiti. Testifying at Mr. Ressam's trial on videotape, Mr. Eugene said he was hired by a documents forger named Leo Kunga, an immigrant from Cameroon, and was paid $150 to drop off the application form and another $150 to pick up the new passport weeks later.

Now Mr. Ressam had a spanking new Canadian identity. With the passport, he was able to get another Social Insurance card, Quebec driver's licence, and Royal Bank Visa card, which he used to purchase the bomb components. He was also able to cross the border with impunity. In March 1998, he flew to Peshawar, Pakistan, met one of Osama bin Laden's top aides, and was ferried to a camp in Afghanistan to learn bomb-making techniques.

While he was away at terrorist training camp, three more warrants were issued for Mr. Ressam's arrest in connection with thefts in British Columbia and Quebec. Despite this, and because of his new identity, he was able to re-enter Canada in February 1999, following his Afghan paramilitary training. He came back via South Korea and Los Angeles. He filled out a Customs Declaration form in the name of Benni Norris.

Mr. Ressam rented another apartment in Montreal. He lived alone, paid his rent in cash, and kept a loaded pistol hidden in his stove. He also opened accounts at the Royal Bank and Bank of Montreal and shopped at Safeway,

Radio Shack, and other stores for the bomb components. He spent around $20,000 before his arrest in December 1999, when he tried to cross the border. Apart from welfare, he had no other known income.

In April 1999, a French antiterrorist investigator asked Ottawa for permission to visit Canada to interview Mr. Ressam and other members of a Montreal jihad cell who were suspected of providing aid to terrorists targeting France. It was not until October that the French were allowed to come. During their visit, the RCMP raided a Montreal apartment occupied by one of the cell members and found an address book containing the coordinates for two of bin Laden's aides. Mr. Ressam's fingerprints were all over the book, but Mr. Ressam could not be found.

In November 1999, he flew to Vancouver and checked into the 2400 Motel with an accomplice from Algeria. They rented room 118 and began mixing the bomb in olive jars. They kept the windows open despite the cold and would not let cleaning staff into the back bedroom. At one point, a chemical spill damaged the kitchenette tabletop and severely burned Mr. Ressam's thigh, according to the allegations.

They checked out of the hotel on December 14 and loaded the explosives into the trunk of a Chrysler 300M, rented from a Thrifty's outlet, and drove to the Tsawwassen ferry terminal, boarding a B.C. Ferries vessel to Schwartz Bay. The accomplice took a Greyhound bus back to Vancouver and got back to Algeria. Meanwhile, Mr. Ressam headed for the car ferry.

In his confession, Mr. Ressam admitted that the plot was hatched in the paramilitary camp in Afghanistan. He was instructed to "take orders" from an Algerian in London and worked closely with dozens of terrorists posing as refugees in Canada. During their stay, they collected welfare and committed crimes to support themselves. They smuggled guns to colleagues, undertook credit card fraud, robbed banks, or shoplifted. They also plotted violent acts.

In January 2002, a *Wall Street Journal* reporter got hold of al-Qaeda secrets on two laptop computers looted by troops in November 2001 from a Taliban office abandoned in Kabul, Afghanistan. The files were undated, but their codes were cracked by high-speed computers. The computer was thought to have been used by bin Laden's right-hand man, Ayman al-Zawahiri, believed to be killed in an air raid. One of the files mentioned a terrorist plot to blow up Israel's embassy buildings in Canada (located in Ottawa, Toronto, and Montreal and guarded by the RCMP). Instructions to cell members were to obtain "preparatory devices for explosives from inside Canada," and also to "gather intelligence about American soldiers who frequent nightclubs" along the Canada–U.S. border as possible targets.

Another frightening plot in Canada was hatched in the summer of 1999 by Ahmed Ressam and other Algerians who wanted to detonate a massive bomb in a bustling neighborhood in Montreal—at Park and Laurier Avenues in Outremont—after seeing Jewish people on the street "with long curly sideburns." This is a Hasidic community neighborhood where some 5,000 ultra-Orthodox Jews live and work in their traditional outfits. Montreal's busy shopping centre, on Ste. Catherine Street, was another target discussed by these Arabs. Instead, they decided to blow up LA Airport on New Year's Eve 1999.

The Ressam court trial, and other investigations into Canadian "refugees" since September 11, revealed the inadequacy of Canada's refugee determination rules and the failure to monitor the activities of newcomers. If Ahmed Ressam and his ilk had been denied entry into Canada in the first place, or deported when they were ordered to be deported, they would never have been able to come so close to executing a massive terrorist attack. Besides that, it was simply luck that Mr. Ressam and his comrades decided against blowing up targets in Canada and murdering hundreds, if not thousands, of innocent Canadians.

Here was the explanation to the Senate in December 2001, by Wade Elcock, the head of the Canadian Security Intelligence Service as to what happened in the Ressam case. It was interesting in light of the fact that

Interpol tipped me off as early as 1997 about the existence in Canada of dozens of dangerous Algerian terrorists. I published the story and nothing happened.

Mr. Elcock: At the end of the day, we do not arrest people. We do not have that capacity. In the case of Mr. Ressam, we were aware that Mr. Ressam had left the country at an earlier period of time ... and we knew where he had gone. We did not know that he had re-entered the country, nor did we know that he had a legitimate passport issued under the name of Benni Norris. He re-entered the country by coming through Los Angeles. At a later time, we had heard rumors that he was back in Canada, in British Columbia. We had not been able to find him, in part, presumably, because we were looking for Ahmed Ressam and not Mr. Benni Norris. Indeed, he had not made contact with people that we were also looking for. At the end of the day, there are risks in this world. Unfortunately, in a democratic state, there are limits to what the police and security services can do. Some people will slip through the net. I would have liked to have found Mr. Ressam before he crossed the border. In the circumstances, we benefitted from what is important in any relationship in any operation to try to reduce the risks of terrorism, a layered defence, if you will. You must have not only good defence and police services but alert border guards and customs officers. All those things in this case dealt with the problem.

Senator LeBreton: Thanks to a woman, an American customs officer, I might add.

The Chairman: Would the situation have been any different had *Bill C-11* [the new *Immigration Act*] been in place at the time? There is a long question at the bottom of page two, which is your testimony on *Bill C-11* before the House committee, in which you said: 'in a perfect world I believe that we would have had sufficient information to advise CIC that Mr. Ressam fell within an 'inadmissible' class of persons. If, again, *Bill C-11* had then been in effect, relevant classified information would have been available to CIC during an admissibility hearing, at the time of entry, during a detention review or appeal before the Immigration Appeal Division.' Can you explain what you could have done had *Bill C-11* been in effect that you could not do beforehand?

Mr. Elcock: Let me read the lines that precede it, and perhaps that will explain it: Under the new Act, the Service would have been involved in front-end screening, and since he arrived with an altered French passport in another name, I believe we would have consulted the French authorities, whom I believe at the time had Ressam's fingerprints, his photograph, and who were aware he had been traveling undercover to and from Corsica in 1993. We are all talking about ifs. Ifs are difficult things at the best of times, but if front-end screening, which is provided for in this legislation, had been in place, there would have been a chance at picking him up earlier rather than later.

An Imported Tragedy

The biggest mass murder in Canadian history involved a terrorist attack against immigrants, believed to have been mounted by immigrants and refugee claimants known to police as problems. On June 23, 1985, Air India Flight #182 disappeared from radar screens while over the Atlantic, as it began its descent to London from Canada. A bomb hidden inside a suitcase and loaded into the belly of the airplane had exploded in its baggage compartment. The aircraft lost control and crashed into the sea. The few who survived the impact of the jet hitting the water drowned in frigid water off the coast of Ireland. The bombing was the most devastating act of aviation terrorism in history. The terrorist attack claimed 329 lives—156 Canadians, 60 children under 10 years of age, and 65 more children between the ages of 11 and 20. Most of them were immigrants too. Among the victims was my daughter's friend, 14-year-old Joti Radhakrishna, her younger brother, and her mother, my daughter's Girl Guides leader.

At exactly the same time as this family and dozens more were blown out of the sky, a bomb inside baggage on a Canadian Airlines flight being transferred to an Air India jet exploded prematurely while on the tarmac of Japan's Narita Airport. The Air India flight was headed for Bangkok. Two baggage handlers were killed. Investigations later revealed that both bombs were built and loaded into the planes while in Canada.

It has been the most complex—and most expensive—investigation ever undertaken in Canadian history. Finally, 15 years later, in October 2000, the RCMP laid charges against three individuals: wealthy Vancouver businessman Ripudaman Singh Malik and Kamloops mill worker Ajaib Bagri. In early February 2001, Duncan, B.C., electrician Inderjit Singh Reyat, while serving a sentence in the Narita bombing, was announced as the third accused in the case. A fourth man, the late Talwinder Singh Parmar, a former Burnaby resident, was described by the RCMP as an unindicted co-conspirator. He was killed by Indian police after being captured there in 1992. Another four Lower Mainland residents are considered suspects in the case, but no further arrests have been made.

The gigantic Air India case, involving a task force of 60 police and dozens of lawyers, has cost taxpayers $50 million so far. There may be 800 witnesses, 170,000 documents with up to a million pages, and years of wiretaps submitted as evidence. Just 131 of the bodies and less than half the plane's wreckage was recovered from the Atlantic Ocean, something that has also hampered the investigation. The trial is expected to begin in 2002—two years after charges were laid—and to last at least six months.

The announced charges were welcomed overwhelmingly by British Columbia's Sikh community of 200,000 persons. The government, and the Air India Task Force prosecutors, were given petitions signed by thousands of Sikh community members who urged judges to deny bail to the accused until the trial. But Sikh violence has plagued them in Canada. Troubles among Sikhs erupted in June 1984, when Indian government soldiers assaulted the Golden Temple, the Sikhs' holiest site, built by one of the religion's earlier gurus, to quell an uprising by a Sikh separatist. Then on October 31, 1984, ethnic tensions were further enflamed when two of Indira Ghandi's Sikh bodyguards gunned her down in revenge for the desecration of the Golden Temple. There was anti-Sikh rioting throughout India. Mobs killed hundreds, and thousands fled to Punjab. The radical organization, the Babbar Khalsa, founded in 1978 in India, had active branches abroad in the United Kingdom and Canada, where large concentrations of Sikhs had immigrated, to further the cause. Another violence-prone group is the International Sikh Youth Federation, also dedicated to turning the Punjab state in India into an independent nation for Sikhs called Khalistan. It has followers in Canada too.

While the vast majority of Sikhs immigrated to Canada in the hopes of a quiet, new life, radical elements exported their violence. These extremists have tried to impose strict observance on Sikhs and to take over temples in order to loot treasuries for terrorist purposes.

Five months after the Air India disaster, police raided a number of homes in Canada and found guns, gunpowder, and dynamite. The late Talwinder Singh Parmar, founder of Babbar Khalsa, was among those being investigated. At the time, he claimed in sermons delivered in Toronto, London, and Vancouver temples that he was being picked on by police in Canada. But he also preached in favor of violence. In 1989, he gave an interview in Punjab threatening Rajiv Ghandi and future Air India passengers.

Both Mr. Parmar and Mr. Reyat, Babbar Khalsa members from Montreal, had previous brushes with the law. They were charged following a joint RCMP–FBI sting for conspiracy to bomb another Air India jet out of New York. An FBI informant and convicted drug trafficker told the FBI that the two agreed to provide a certain large amount of heroin in return for a bomb to be put on a flight. The two were convicted in 1986, appealed, and eventually had their charges dismissed on the grounds that their

Charter rights were violated because it took six years for a retrial to commence. There was no attempt to deport them.

By 1987, the two had left Canada, Mr. Reyat for the U.K. and Mr. Parmar for Pakistan, where he crossed into India. Mr. Reyat was eventually extradited from Britain and in 1991 was found guilty of two counts of manslaughter in the Narita Airport bomb blast. He has been serving a 10-year sentence.

Tamil Terrorists

Another secession movement, in the island nation of Sri Lanka, has cost 60,000 lives in the last 17 years and displaced one million people. It is Asia's bloodiest and longest-running current war. The nation's ethnic minority, the Tamils, have been involved in violent attacks in their efforts to separate. They are Hindu and number 3.2 million in a population of 18.7 million, of which the majority are Buddhist Sinhalese. This rivalry has been exported to Canada, where major fundraising efforts have been mounted in the 1990s.

The resistance began under a democratic political party, but was taken over in the early 1980s by the militant and separatist Liberation Tigers of Tamil Eelam (LTTE). The group has waged a campaign of terror, recruiting child soldiers and teenage girls, who are brainwashed into becoming suicide bombers. It has blown up hundreds of civilians, dozens of Sinhalese politicians, and scores of moderate Tamil leaders. In 1994, President Chandrika Kumaratunga offered the LTTE a devolution package. It refused. In 1999, she was re-elected, barely escaping an assassination attempt in which she lost an eye. The war costs the country $1 billion a year in security measures and damages.

Canada has become key for the Tamils, whose diaspora in Canada, centered in Toronto, is the largest outside Sri Lanka. Between 150,000 and 250,000 in number, most came in as refugee claimants. Funds are collected by an umbrella organization called FACT, the Federation of Associations of Canadian Tamils, and the World Tamil Movement. Both are listed by the U.S. State Department as front organizations for the LTTE, which is branded a terrorist organization.

It has long been illegal in the U.S. to raise funds for the Tigers, but not in Canada, until antiterrorist legislation was imposed after September 11. FACT has received government grants to do immigrant settlement work. This prompted critics to accuse Ottawa of naïveté, of legitimizing the Tigers' political arm, helping it raise between $12 million and $22 million a year. Tamils say they are not fomenting violence in Canada, and that their money looks after causes and victims.

Sri Lankan militants realized that Canada was an easy mark. Once inside the country as refugees, many set up a consultancy business to help others get here. Printed instructions as to how to lie and what to say were distributed by these people-smugglers back in Sri Lanka. Their systematic exploitation of our refugee and immigration system led to some spectacularly successful results.

Even more outrageous was that Canadian refugee officials did nothing to enforce rules that allow the revocation of refugee status if the "refugee" goes back home to the place he or she allegedly fled. But Canadian officials said that more than 8,600 Sri Lankans with refugee claims pending in Canada applied for travel documents to visit Sri Lanka in 1992. The following year the figure was 5,865.

An estimated 30 top Tamil militants, and others connected with terrorist organizations, live in Toronto.

Canada's permissiveness actually encourages problems, it doesn't relieve them. This applies not only in the case of the Tamils, but also in the case of other terrorist groups who flourish here. In fact, Sri Lankan stateswoman Chandrika Kumaratunga has blamed Canada in international forums for aiding and abetting Tamil Tigers by providing a refuge and funding base.

"There is no distinction between the terrorists who devastated U.S. targets on September 11 and the Tamil tigers who attacked Sri Lanka's international airport this past July," she said in a speech in November 2001, "or who, in just the last few weeks, rammed an oil tanker in our waters and tried to assassinate our Prime Minister. It is time for the international community to close ranks and take practical and meaningful action to eradicate terrorism.

"The Tigers have offices in Toronto, London, Paris, and New Jersey. They draw on the "misguided loyalties" of the global Tamil diaspora of 450,000 to 500,000 people, mostly in North America, Europe, and Australia. They exploit large Tamil communities in places such as Canada to obtain funds and supplies for its fighters in Sri Lanka. The Tamil Tigers simply cannot be allowed to abuse democratic freedoms by raising money in Canada and elsewhere for the bombs and bullets used to murder our people," Ms. Kumaratunga said.

Former Canadian High Commissioner in Sri Lanka, Martin Collacott, also provided the background to the growth of cells in Canada. "Support from Canadian sources has been a major factor in nurturing the vicious and bloody campaign of terrorism being waged by the Tamil Tigers in Sri Lanka. What is surprising and disturbing is that some Canadian leaders still refuse to admit that by cultivating the Federation of Associations of Canadian Tamils—a key front organization for the Tigers in Canada—they continue to encourage funding that has, in large measure, made possible the insurgency and acts of terror that have killed tens of thousands of Sri Lankans.

"When I served as Canadian High Commissioner to Sri Lanka from 1982 to 1986, the period in which civil war began in earnest, I urged the Sri Lankan government to redress Tamil grievances and worked actively to ensure that Canadian aid (and particularly our large-scale involvement in irrigation programs) was used to benefit the Tamils as well as the other races. I visited the Tamil heartland in Jaffna immediately after the anti-

Tamil riots in 1983 and again in 1986, at a time when no other high commissioners or ambassadors went there to demonstrate their concern for the Tamil population. Having said this, I now must say I am appalled by the way in which the Tamil Tigers and their supporters have abused and exploited Canadian hospitality," he said.

"Few recent terrorist movements have matched the brutality and ruthlessness of the Liberation Tigers of Tamil Eelam. Their bombs, which have killed hundreds of innocent civilians, have been designed to sow terror among the population as well as try to precipitate a violent reaction against Tamils in order to give substance to allegations that they are being persecuted by the Sri Lankan government (a claim which, *inter alia*, has enabled large numbers of Tiger members and supporters to claim refugee status in Canada). A particular trademark of the Tigers, and one that reveals their true character, has been their systematic murder of moderate Tamil leaders in an effort to ensure that the Tigers and their extremist supporters enjoy total dominance and control over the community," he added.

"While the Tigers have not committed outright acts of terrorism in Canada, they and their accomplices have been involved in a wide range of criminal activities in this country in addition to the extortion of huge payments from Tamils here. [Criminal activities] include drug trafficking, migrant smuggling, passport forgery, and fraud. They have also been a major factor in the spawning of Tamil street gangs in Toronto, which have accounted for 40 shootings in the past three years and five unsolved homicides," he said.

Welcome to Club Fed

The majority of immigrants, like native-borns, are hard-working and honest. But Canada's naïve laws, its lax immigration policies, and its reluctance to deport anyone, have attracted organized crime figures from around the world, say police sources. Italian Mafia figures immigrated along with hundreds of thousands of hard-working Italian immigrants after the Second World War. After the demise of the Soviet Union, Russians and other Eastern European mobsters began arriving as refugee claimants or as investor immigrants with millions of dollars. Ironically, one of Canada's biggest attractions for them are our high-quality jails. When nabbed for shoplifting or car theft, the petty criminals in these organizations simply plead guilty and do their time. "They love our prisons and can still do business on cell phones while serving their time. And we feed them, let them in free, and never deport them," said a member of an elite police squad in Toronto that specializes in Eastern European criminality.

A story in a Toronto newspaper about this quoted a conversation that took place between a man in a Canadian prison and another in Russia. "You must come to Canada. This is a wonderful place. I'm in jail and eat meat three times a day," he said.

"Meat?" asked his friend.

Responded the Canadian convict: "Yes, three times a day."

Another pause, and then the other man, sounding almost awed, asked: "Meat and potatoes?"

Canadian convict: "Yes. You should come here and commit a crime."

Police said that 150,000 calls were monitored from one cell phone during a six-month period and that 60 crimes a week were planned on average. "These guys have several going at once. They literally deal with everything from assassinations to shoplifting. They simply don't give a s—. They just do it."

Another Russian crime expert, RCMP Inspector David Douglas, was quoted in 1999 as saying, "There's no doubt Canada is a pretty good spot for these guys. Access into the country is relatively easy. Deportation takes a while, as everybody knows. There also seems to be some ease in moving money, money laundering, through this country. So they've picked Canada for a reason."

Others allowed into Canada include members of Chinese triads and Vietnamese gangs, plus bikers from south of the border who are involved in the drug business in Vancouver and elsewhere.

After September 11, and now that al-Qaeda cells operating in Canada have been identified, the American public is realizing what its police forces have known: Canada's immigration, refugee, and legal system facilitates the entry into the continent of organized crime groups and terrorists.

"Unless and until Canada can tighten its controls on immigration and refugees, these controls will have to be imposed at the border," said one of America's top experts on terrorism and crime, Buck Revell, in an interview shortly after the 9–11 attacks. "You [Canada] are amongst the problems, and if the problem is not solved, we're going to have a different circumstance along the border. Canadians should understand that this is not about turning our backs on Canada but about a vulnerability in Canada that, if it isn't addressed by Canada, must be addressed by the United States."

Mr. Revell is a Dallas-based terrorist and crime consultant and served as second-in-command at the Federal Bureau of Investigation until the mid-1990s. He serves as an advisor to Washington's Task Force on Transnational Threats. While with the FBI, he masterminded its attack on the Italian Mafia with policing and legislative tools devised to track and confiscate assets.

"Washington has great concern about Canada. They see what's happening here. We obviously have our own problems, but Canada's been an easy mark for years. Law enforcement there is very frustrated with the growth of the organized criminal elements and concerned that the terrorist groups realize Canada's a fertile ground, not only in terms of getting in and staying but also for fundraising and propaganda and other financial services," he said.

Mr. Revell believes that one major reform the Canadian government must undertake in this war against terrorists is to merge its intelligence gathering agency, CSIS, back with the RCMP. The two were separated in the 1970s, after political pressure following the separatist crisis in the late 1960s led to the McDonald Commission. "The RCMP in particular, since then, has lost its intelligence function and feels it's operating in the blind. In the

States, the FBI has both counterterrorist and criminal investigation knitted together in one agency. This allows the FBI to quickly get up to speed as to who and what to look at. We saw this benefit in the World Trade Center and McVeigh cases."

In contrast, Canada took 15 years to arrest suspects after the biggest terrorist act in Canadian history—the bombing of the Air India jetliner.

"Concern about Canada really goes back to the prior era of Armenian and Sikh, Croatian and a number of other European organizations that were operating in North America. We found that almost all of them came in through Canada, even though a majority of attacks were against the U.S.," he said. "We had also noted in the arena of organized crime not only Italians, also Chinese triads, Korean criminals and yakuza [Japanese gangsters]. Many of them were entering the United States through Canada. This started us in a dialogue with the RCMP. They candidly acknowledged at the time there was virtually no control over entry into Canada or whether people stayed beyond visa requirements and that the police had very little they could do about it because of the politicians."

He said that in the famous Pizza Connection Mafia case, criminals moved freely from Sicily to Canada then south. That's when the FBI realized that Canada was a "vulnerability."

"Our unguarded border should stay that way, but we started expressing concerns about the fact that, even when we identified and brought charges against people, we had a difficult time getting them extradited," he said. "There should be seamless extradition. If we are going to have open borders, we must have compatible and co-ordinated criminal justice systems."

Oliver Twist, Honduran-Style

The Colombian drug cartels have also been able to establish direct "marketing" efforts, thanks to our refugee determination system and the abdication of protection. In 1999, I was called by an undercover policeman in Vancouver to write about how the Colombian drug cartels were using Canada's refugee system to peddle heroin to Canadians. He was furious at the federal government for allowing them into the country and letting them stay. We drove up and down the streets and back alleys of Vancouver's skid row in the city's east end. Here, he said, scores of fake refugees control the city's drug trade, ruining Canadian lives with narcotics that are more affordable, and more addictive, than ever. For two hours we drove around, observing the scene. In an alley, a man picked through a dumpster behind a restaurant. There was litter everywhere. Old sleeping bags, towels, pieces of clothing. Small bottles of bleach, used by addicts to disinfect their needles, sat on doorsteps. Still, the neighborhood was afflicted by one of the country's highest incidences of AIDS.

A member of a drug squad, the policeman could not go public for fear of losing his job, but he wanted Canadians to know how the refugee system failed to protect our society. Hundreds of Honduran teenagers arrived in Vancouver during the late 1990s, making false claims as "refugees" and getting away with it. They were brought in by the Colombian drug cartels and worked off their "debt" by peddling narcotics. Their gangster masters were in Canada, too, as refugees.

"In two years, the Hispanics, who are all here under the refugee program, have taken over the crack business," explained the policeman. "Crack is the drug of choice. The high is so intense that people are hooked right from the start. Five years ago, the Vancouver city police found it hard to find a rock of crack. Not any more. It's everywhere. The Hispanics are putting more and more pure stuff on the street."

Heroin was the same story. "It's only $10 to $15 for a hit of heroin these days, the supply's so great," he said. "Kids are smoking heroin in high schools. It's as easy to get heroin now as it is to order a pizza. In no time, they may have a $300- to $500-a-day habit. How do they pay for it? Prostitution, crime, or by dealing drugs themselves, spreading the addiction to others. The misery is exponential."

The Honduran drug dealers were highly visible. Deals were being done in front of convenience stores, restaurants, and the Skytrain station. The Hondurans all wore a "uniform"—baggy designer jeans, Nike shoes, slinky soccer shirts, and gold chains. They worked in shifts and in pairs. One negotiated. The other, often only 10 or 11 years of age, carried "spitballs" or plastic sacks of crack in his mouth. The young men were victims, too. In September 1999, an 11-year-old Honduran refugee accidentally swallowed his spitballs when chased by police and nearly died of an overdose.

Most of the dealers I observed that night had girlfriends, obviously a native-born Canadians, in tow. These girls get hooked on drugs, have sex with the dealers, and often become pregnant, explained the policeman. This way, the dealers can remain in Canada more easily because they have a Canadian child and can appeal to the immigration minister for leave to stay on humanitarian grounds.

The policeman explained that most of the dealers were recruited from the slums of Honduras with newspaper advertisements that boasted, "Come to Canada and make big money." Once here, the young men were coached on how to apply as refugees, get welfare, and do business. "It's easy," says the police officer. "You come in [as a visitor, with or without a visa, by plane, car, or illegally] and go to the Immigration office to make a claim to stay as a refugee. You have no documents. So you are sent to a clerk who types out a 1442 immigration document, called Notice to Seek Refugee Claim. You tell the clerk your name. She types it. You make up your date of birth, country of origin, occupation, bio. She types it all in. She calls a commissionaire, and he takes you and your 1442 to another place to take your fingerprints. You walk out as a fictitious character.

"Next stop is Employment Canada. The 1442 is presented, and the clerk there issues a Social Insurance Number card. With that piece of identification, a provincial ID card can be obtained, entitling holders to welfare, health care, and any other benefits, such as emergency loans for housing purposes and so on. In hours, you have created a new identity."

Most of these boys and young men live Dickensian lives as drug-dealing Oliver Twists who are enslaved to the cocaine cartels' dangerous and demanding Fagins. In a recent raid, there were 30 boys living in a tiny apartment. Most eventually get hooked on the lifestyle of a drug dealer. Some end up getting hooked on the drugs themselves.

The Hondurans first emerged in California and Oregon, where an intense crackdown in the mid-1990s led to the deportation of 7,000 in 2001. This drove an unknown number to British Columbia and other parts of Canada. Meanwhile, even if caught in Canada, refugee lawyers have often successfully plea-bargained suspended sentences for these young men on the basis that a conviction and jail sentence would impede their refugee claim and lead to deportation. Of those deported, many may return as refugees under an assumed identity or live, as drug dealers and crooks, beneath the radar screen.

"The drug cartels were bringing up 13 and 15 year olds to be mules and pushers," said Vancouver Mayor Philip Owen in an interview with me in 2001. Hundreds came into Canada, and few have been deported. They live on welfare payments and illegal drug receipts, spreading their "product" beyond the city's slummier, drug-infested neighborhood. "They are deported, and they would come back three and four times and reapply as refugee claimants."

"It's not unusual to pick up a guy in Vancouver and find out he's been deported and returned four or five times," said a Vancouver police department detective specializing in bank robbery investigations in an interview in August 2001. "What we're finding is that whether they go to jail or not, they go to school on crime and come out able to undertake even bigger crimes, such as frauds, or bank robberies, or drug trafficking."

Student Visa Scams

Canadian immigration authorities abroad have also badly botched up the visa-granting process. Not only are the systems' visa officers vulnerable to bribes, threats, and nepotism, as malfeasance figures reveal, but they are simply swamped. Student visas are an easy, backdoor way to gain entry, in both the U.S. and Canada. This is because they are easily forged, educational institutions often vouch for applicants, and there is never any follow-up after the term has expired. In August 1999, I obtained an internal report from an Immigration Department source who was upset that nothing was being done about the fact that organized crime groups in China were providing false documentation so that unqualified people could fraudulently obtain student visas. The report, called *Chinese Student Visas: Evidence of Organized Fraud*, showed that two-thirds of the applications recently investigated involved "systematic, organized fraud." These people did not have the financial means to attend school in Canada, nor were they really interested in studying.

A Canadian diplomat in Beijing, Susan Gregson heads the immigration section, and she confirmed that applications in Beijing for student visas were skyrocketing, up by 179 per cent. Some 2,273 visas were granted in 1999, compared to only 689 granted in 1997. "I'm not aware of the exact report, but two-thirds organized fraud? That sounds reasonable," she said in a telephone interview from Beijing. "In a disturbingly high number of cases we have checked, we find that the parents are not working where they say they are working or it's a rundown place that simply couldn't give them the income they are allegedly earning. False documentation is so easily available here. There has grown up a whole industry of Chinese immigration agents who provide, as part of their service, fraudulent documents. This is the minority of cases we believe, but I don't have the resources to check out every application."

Once in Canada, nobody tracks the whereabouts of the students or what they are doing. And nobody ensures that they return on the date when their visas expire. Nobody knows how many never left and have disappeared or changed identities. In 2000, the deaths of three Canadians were linked to persons who had stayed in Canada after their student visas had expired. The principal of a private school in Mississauga that catered to Chinese visa students was kidnapped, held for ransom, and then murdered. Two of his former students, both on visas, were charged with first-degree murder, kidnapping, extortion, forcible confinement, and robbery. Another case involved the death of two infants whose Japanese mother had been illegally in Canada for years. One toddler starved to death and the other infant disappeared. The mother was wanted on a deportation order by Immigration officials for years.

A Country at Risk

Former FBI chief Buck Revell is correct; Americans have a right to be concerned about Canada's porous border. But so do ordinary Canadians who continue to fall victim to persons who should never have been accepted into Canada in the first place and, having been discovered as undesirable or dangerous, should never have been allowed to stay. But they are rarely, if ever, removed. At the end of 2001, there were 27,000 unserved deportation orders in Canada. Here are some examples that have hit the press in the past few years.

Iranian terrorist Mansour Ahani, a trained assassin, neatly avoided deportation for eight years by invoking every legal technicality available, at a cost of millions to taxpayers. He was finally ordered deported by the Supreme Court of Canada in early January 2002. The high court ruled he was a danger to Canadian security, had been given a fair chance to appeal his case, and had not demonstrated he faced torture in Iran.

But immigration officials gave him 72 hours to make travel arrangements. That was enough time to allow him to obtain a temporary halt from a Toronto judge pending an appeal. Then he undertook a series of last-ditch legal proceedings. His lawyer turned to the UN for a ruling and spent the rest of the winter unsuccessfully arguing in the lower courts that Canada, as a signatory to the UN Covenant on Civil and Political Rights, should let Ahani stay until the UN issues a decision. After losing in the Ontario Court of Appeal, Ahani tried again to go to the Supreme Court of Canada, to argue that his *Charter of Rights* guarantee of fundamental justice was being violated by the government's attempts to send him to Iran before the UN committee made its ruling. A three-judge panel refused to hear the case. There was one dissent. Amnesty International condemned the Canadian governments' refusal to wait for the UN pronouncement before sending him home. He was finally deported in June 2002.

Such delay, not to mention the expense, in deporting Mr. Ahani is unjustifiable, given the fact that he was a member of the Iranian state security forces and became a hit man. He flew to Vancouver in October 1991 and claimed refugee status. Then he settled in Toronto and resumed his work as a secret agent. What crimes, if any, he committed here on Canadian soil against Canadians or others is unknown. But it is known that he traveled to Italy at the request of Iran with the sole purpose of killing a pro-democracy dissident. He did not murder that person, but returned to Canada, where he was arrested in 1993 as a threat to national security. He has been kept in a Hamilton jail ever since.

Another case involves Somalian warlord Mahmoud Mohammad Issa Mohammad. He was convicted in 1968 of participating in an attack by the Popular Front for the Liberation of Palestine against an El Al plane in Athens, in which one person died. After serving only four months in prison, he was released when his fellow terrorists hijacked an airplane and held its 155 passengers hostage until his release.

"The PLO negotiated his release," said an immigration official. "He went to Spain, assumed a new identity, and came to Canada in 1987. We found out he was here. We instituted deportation hearings against him, and he is still here. He's living happily in Brantford, and his case is still before the courts."

One obstacle is that by 1987, he had become a landed immigrant in Canada because he had lied about his past and withheld the fact that he was a fugitive. Deportation proceedings started in 1988, and his defence, successful to date, has been that his release from Greek prison constituted a full pardon. He also made a refugee claim in 1989 as a Plan B, in case deportation was ordered. After making a mockery of Canada's Immigration department, Mr. Mohammad's Federal Court appeal date had still not been set at the end of 2001.

Criminals are difficult to eject from our society. José Fernandes from Portugal was ordered deported on February 14, 1985, after an immigration inquiry was held into his multiple criminal convictions involving violence. He was not fit to live here, and under the *Immigration Act*, as it existed then, he should have been kicked out. He successfully appealed his deportation, and after many adjournments a hearing was held in January 1986. He was not deported until 1995, after he had committed more criminal acts.

In 1985, he was 25 years of age, had married a Canadian citizen, and had become the father of two young children. The Immigration Appeal Board stayed the deportation order and said he could remain if he behaved for three years. In June 1989, the board was informed that Fernandes had been convicted of another criminal offence. Nevertheless, on December 13, 1989, the Board gave him another two years to behave. But more convictions occurred, and another hearing was called in March 1989. Mr. Fernandes didn't even bother to show up, so the board refused his appeal to extend the stay, thus essentially ordering him deported. In April 1992, the board was asked to reopen the case because Fernandes said his failure to attend was beyond his control. A hearing on this matter was set for September, 1992. More adjournments followed.

Finally, a date of August 1993 was set for a hearing. Eventually, a hearing was held in May 1994 in the Collins Bay Institution, a prison where Fernandes was incarcerated. After more submissions, the Immigration Appeal Division ended its stay order in September 1994—nine years after the original order to deport. It was then appealed to the Federal Court, which upheld the Immigration Appeal Division decision to get rid of him.

During his adult life, Fernandes had a record of 40 convictions (assault, break and enter, possession of a weapon, assaulting a police officer, theft, and mischief) between 1977 and 1993. He had been given several reprieves in return for promises to rehabilitate. Evidence was that he could rehabilitate. He did not do so. Along the way, Fernandes's lawyers (paid for under legal aid with taxpayers' dollars) argued under the *Charter of Rights and Freedoms* that his children had a right not to be deprived of their father. They argued that deportation was cruel and unusual punishment. But the board said

1. The right to remain in Canada is conditional and is absolute only in the case of Canadian citizens.
2. Deportation is not cruel and unusual punishment.
3. There was no exceptional status applicable to a long-term permanent resident.
4. The board said there was nothing preventing the wife and children from joining him in Portugal, so their rights were unaffected.

Obviously the case dragged on for far too long, but at least the corrective action was taken. Not so in the case involving José Salinas-Mendoza who arrived in Canada in 1988 from El Salvador and claimed refugee status. While on welfare, Mendoza committed many crimes and was convicted of 12 offences, ranging from drunken driving to sexual assault and assault. In September 1993, he was charged with rape, and charges were stayed on condition that he be deported. He was escorted back to El Salvador. In April 1994, he arrived back in Canada and was able to successfully claim refugee status again. In May 1994, he was arrested for other crimes, but released from custody and told to appear in court in June 1994. That court did not know that he had been charged with rape and that the charges had been stayed only because he was deported.

While running around our society free, without bail, this violent man was spotted by the victim he had raped years before. He was arrested in May and was ordered to be incarcerated by an immigration official, until a refugee hearing in August 1994. One month later, his former rape charges were relaid in criminal court. But two days later, another immigration adjudicator in British Columbia released him. His current whereabouts are unknown.

Not removing persons who are convicted of offences is just inviting expenses or tragedies. One of the worst, which occurred in 1999, involved a retired high school principal who volunteered with Scouts Canada. That December, Jim Lindala, 63, and his wife, Viola, were at Toronto's airport on their way to a dream two-week cruise in Hawaii. As he was unloading their luggage from the back of the family van he was hit by an airport limousine that careened up the ramp and crushed him from behind.

"Instead of stopping, the limo hit my husband and pushed us 18 feet down the road," said Viola, who was sitting in the van at the time. "Jim started yelling for an ambulance. His leg had been severed."

He went into a coma. The limo driver, charged with careless driving, had been ordered deported seven years before. Mohammad T. Belfetey-mouri Shafi, an Iranian, requested refugee status in 1989, but was ordered deported in 1995 after he was convicted of assault and mischief in May 1992. He was sentenced to four months' imprisonment. Mr. Lindala lost his leg, had a stroke, and was paralyzed.

Shafi was charged after the accident and fined a mere $365. The court reduced the fine to $300 and said the driver could not lose points or his driver's license because the incident occurred on private property, i.e., the airport is owned by the federal government. An alert police officer on duty at the airport asked the Immigration Department to run a check on his name, turning up Shafi's record. Shafi was then arrested by immigration officers and released following a detention review. According to limo drivers, he is still working in Toronto.

Deportation to some countries is made all the more difficult if there is not a reciprocal agreement in place to handle such cases. Countries of origin often balk. Guyana was a case in point, and fought in Canadian courts the return of several convicted persons on the basis that they had citizenship but had not been raised in Guyana, but in Canada of Guyanese parents. In that case, immigration officials accompanied the people on the flight and simply delivered them there against the wishes of the government.

Even when there is an extradition treaty or agreements, Canadian officialdom sometimes fumbles the ball. Toronto police were outraged in February 2002 that a violent fugitive who was deported to Jamaica from the U.S. for sex offences was granted refugee status after slipping into Canada. Tafari Rennock, 23, was arrested by Toronto police in June 2001 for being in Canada illegally, and turned over to immigration officials. While in custody, Rennock filed a refugee claim, which was accepted by an Immigration and Refugee Board (IRB) even though it was told that he had been deported from the U.S. two years before following convictions for burglary, drug trafficking, robberies, unlawful restraint, probation violations, and a vicious sexual attack on a woman.

Canada's industry of immigration lawyers has also gotten wealthier by asking Canadian courts to judge the laws of other countries and, by so doing, turning fugitives into "refugees." In 1999, a Colombian refugee was deported from Nova Scotia seven years after breaking the law. He delayed deportation because his wife agreed to sponsor him. Then he assaulted her twice, and she withdrew the offer. It still took years to get rid of him. That same year, a Canadian court ruled that a convicted pedophile/refugee could stay here permanently, after having been ordered deported. Yet another undesirable allowed to stay was Oleg Velitchko, a

31-year-old "kickboxer" from Belarus, who was given a five-year sentence in June 1997 for extortion and assault. At the time, immigration officials said they would decide if he should be deported, but they did nothing. Then, in May 1998, Velitchko was sentenced to another four years for assault, obstruction of justice, uttering threats, breaking a court order, and theft.

Even if refugee claimants have been caught defrauding the system, they are not automatically deported as is the practice in most other countries. A former U.S. fugitive with three wives, Navteg Singh Sanghera, aka Tagjinder Singh, was convicted in the U.S. of attempted murder in the stabbing of a 15-year-old boy in Seattle in 1985. The victim was left to die. Mr. Sanghera used a phony name to get into Canada and filed a refugee claim. He then married a Brampton woman in an effort to obtain status here. That meant he had broken a number of laws already—fraudulent documentation and bigamy—and yet he wasn't deported until 1998.

Likewise, a Federal Court judge ruled in 1999 that a Russian man who lied about his criminal convictions when he entered Canada cannot be considered a danger to the public. Edouard Aronovich Bakchiev, a 45-year-old resident of Surrey, B.C., came to Canada as a refugee claimant in 1992 and was granted permanent resident status a year later, even though it was discovered that he had failed to mention to Canadian officials that he had spent more than a decade in prison in Dagestan for armed robbery, and weapons and drug offences. That should have been automatic grounds for deportation, as in other places, but not in Canada.

This country's generosity toward criminals knows few bounds. In 1999, Guyanese immigrant Sunil Bhagwandass, with a series of convictions for drug trafficking, break and enter, and robbery, was allowed to remain in Canada as a refugee. In 1995, a Federal Court judge overturned a deportation order against Jordanian criminal Nedal Mohammed Ibrahim, who had repaid Canada's hospitality by robbing gas stations. Ibrahim's lawyer, David Matas, subsequently appeared before the United Nations Human Rights Commission, with financial support from Canadian taxpayers, to argue that the removal of non-citizens guilty of serious criminal offences, to countries where they might be tortured or executed was a violation of the Universal Declaration of Human Rights, to which Canada is a signatory.

While courts bend over backward for refugees who commit hideous crimes here, they have no sympathy for their Canadian victims. In 1999, a London, Ontario, woman who was raped in 1993 by a criminal facing a deportation order tried to sue the government for negligence because it did not protect her from her assailant. The judge dismissed the woman's $1 million lawsuit, saying immigration authorities made reasonable steps to deport Michael Philip, who had been under a stayed removal order since 1988. Philip, 42, a landed immigrant from Trinidad, was under the removal order because of earlier convictions for sexual assault and wife-beating. In 1993, years later, he attacked the woman.

Another judge in 2000 granted a reprieve to a drug trafficker with AIDS who was facing deportation, saying he was not treated fairly when declared a danger to the public. In overturning the decision that declared Jesus Cristobal of Vancouver, 43, a danger, the judge found it would be "more in keeping with the principles of fairness and natural justice" to give the man a chance to respond to the finding that he was a public danger because of the "profound significance" it has had on his life.

Similarly, a Sikh student, who got early release after 10 years in jail for his part in an Air India hijacking, came to Canada illegally and hid for eight months before being arrested. He was ordered deported, but his family had obtained a pardon from Pakistan (where the hijacking occurred), and a Canadian federal court judge ruled that he should not be deported because "it would be a grave assault on the Canadian sense of justice" since he had been cleansed of his conviction through the pardon.

Even when we order someone deported, there are problems. Most people are asked to voluntarily leave and no follow-up is done. But one case reported to me involved a man in custody who eluded removal. In October 2001, he was booked on a charter flight from Toronto to Jamaica. An immigration official showed up with the man, who had just been released from jail. He was checked in, received his boarding pass and was escorted through security, but failed to reach the gate or board the flight. He should have been personally accompanied back to Jamaica, which is what other countries do. He was not.

"The procedure is that you are supposed to wait until the door of the plane is shut," said former Immigration and Refugee Board lawyer Elizabeth Dodd in an interview in 2001. "But they are rarely accompanied. Sometimes they are drugged or sedated but, even so, many pilots have refused to fly deportees if they are violent. One Jamaican in Vancouver put his foot through plexiglass in the waiting room, and the pilot said no way. He was taken back."

Horror Stories from inside the Refugee Board

A Board Member

Professor Lubomyr Luciuk was a member of the Immigration and Refugee Board from 1996 to 1998. An author of history books on refugees and a professor at the Royal Military College in Kingston, he enthusiastically accepted a posting as a member in Toronto in the hopes that he could, in some small way, help refugees escape tyranny as his two parents had done. Two years later, he left the board thoroughly disillusioned and cynical. "I thought all the problems were naïveté and the fact that some people in the department were just trying to be goody-goody. But I've become convinced that this refugee mess is the policy of the Liberal government. My first indication of the problems was during my initial hearings involving young Tamil men, when the translator turned to me and said 'they're all lying through their teeth.'"

In October 2001, after the September 11 terrorist attacks, he wrote a cynical piece about how to become a refugee that appeared in many newspapers across the country. It was designed to alert the public to the dangers of open-ended migration through the refugee loophole. It sparked an interesting debate in the letters to the editor columns of newspapers, which follow:

"How to be a Refugee in Canada. Be a liar. That's the first lesson learned by most claimants who come before the Immigration and Refugee Board. How? Well, first of all, bring no identity documents, or use fake ones. Be vague about who you are, where you came from, how you got here and, most of all, about why you left. Except, of course, for repeatedly insisting that you face nothing less than torture or even martyrdom if you return. Repeat this mantra. Practise looking downcast. Cry. Unless you are an utter imbecile, you stand an excellent chance of getting refugee status in Canada.

"Getting here probably wasn't difficult. Assert otherwise. Remember, you are a victim. Even so, by the date of your hearing, be composed. By then you will have savoured several months, perhaps years, of the privileges Canadians enjoy without attendant responsibilities. This boon comes courtesy of a Supreme Court that ruled in 1985 that you and yours should enjoy the full protection of our *Charter of Rights and Freedoms*. That turned Canada into a haven for people just like you. And assorted terrorists, drug peddlers and war criminals.

"Don't worry about your hearing. You will leave amazed at how many contortions Canadians will go through to ensure you stay. Still, there are things you should do. First, ask for a delay, several times. Get a note from a compatriot to let the board know you have been gravely ill. Why delay? Because you accumulate the maximum amount of welfare. That helps pay off the smugglers who got you here. Paying your debts can be stressful, especially when you are a stranger in a strange land. But look at the positive side. By being here you are already better off than you could ever have been where you came from. You're earning dollars. And if you have medical problems, we'll fix you up. No charge. Canadians can wait.

"Hiring legal counsel is no problem. True, a lot of crooks masquerade as immigration consultants, but don't worry. Canada's taxpayers guarantee you

Legal Aid. You can afford the appropriate pettifogger. When your big day at the board comes, accept only a two-member panel. You stand a much better chance of admission, for if one goes negative and the other positive, you're in. You always get the benefit of the doubt. Hey, you have more rights than a Canadian. Granted, you may be anxious. You've been telling fibs all along. What if someone catches on? Don't worry. The board's members are only human. They are not really required to explain a positive determination, but they must justify a negative one, which can be appealed to the federal court. So most members go positive, most of the time. It is nicer that way.

"True, some members specialize in reserving decisions. Don't worry if that happens. When their writing backlogs grow they get time off to catch up. Wanting out of the hearing rooms is perfectly understandable. Imagine how tedious it is listening to the same story, day after day. Most members have heard your fable, or some minor variant of it, many times before. Their main job is to pretend they haven't and make it look as if they did not prejudge your claim. Of course, they have. With most members you're in, facts and your false witness notwithstanding.

"New members do occasionally wonder why so many claimants' stories sound so much alike. There's a simple answer. Remember the smugglers who brought you to Canada? They weren't exactly Hollywood scriptwriters, were they? They coached you in what tale you should recite, like thousands before you. Stick to the script! Should you mess up, immediately claim to be suffering post-traumatic stress disorder. The board members will feel your pain. If you happen to belong to one of several racial, ethnic or religious minorities the board mollycoddles, you're lucky. For example, if you're a Tamil, male and "young" (no exact definition exists, for being precise is considered discriminatory) you will likely appear before a panel that agrees you fit the "profile" of a person at risk in Sri Lanka. Basically, that means everyone. So welcome to Canada, after only the most perfunctory screening. Reportedly we now have quite a sub-population of young, male Tamil Tiger terrorists in Canada, courtesy of the IRB.

"At the board there are those who don't want Canadians to hear any of this. They enjoy their perks and wallow in notions of their importance. They dismiss those who, like me, accepted an appointment to the board out of a desire to help refugees but ended up utterly disillusioned by the determination process. To silence critics, they defame us as anti-refugee, anti-immigrant, xenophobic. Balderdash. But I do concede that I had a problem at the board. I rarely encountered a real refugee there, and so I was labelled 'Dr. No' for handing down negative decisions on more than 90 per cent of the claims before me. Those who blackballed me didn't care that my parents were political refugees who fled Nazi and communist tyranny.

"Like true refugees from anywhere, my folks shared a compulsive need to return home. Remarkably few claimants at the IRB said they'd rather be back home. They just talked about how bad it was there and how happy they could be here. As I listened to their yarns, I realized the overwhelming majority organized their own shipment to Canada for economic reasons. Some are good people who had hard lives or faced discrimination, a few much worse. But most did not have a well-founded fear of persecution. So I had no choice but to become 'Dr. No.'

"Now I'm glad I was. For I also became 'Dr. Know.' Unlike our blinkered Immigration Minister, Elinor Caplan, and her minions, I know that if the IRB continues as it has then just about anyone who wants to get into Canada will get in. And our country will disappear as surely as New York City's twin towers vanished in the holocaust orchestrated by the terrorists who wormed their way in amongst us, courtesy of lax immigration laws. Many more remain, undetected, to our peril."

Reaction to his piece, which ran in many newspapers, was swift. Gertrud Neuwirth, Carleton University Professor of Sociology and Director of Research for the school's Division of Refugees, waded in first. Canada's acceptance rate of refugees was 45 percent of applicants, according to United Nations figures—"a number less than one-tenth of 1 percent of the total population."

She said that Canada's refugee policy should not be linked to the September 11 terrorist acts because the culprits entered the United States directly as tourists or on visas. As for claimants lying or using fake documents or arriving without documents, she said this was in keeping with the fact that they come from countries where identity papers are either not used or destroyed. She asked, Can you expect people to ask for a passport from a country they are fleeing? Maybe they can get out only with fake identity. She added that stress leads to fabrications and that stories among claimants are the same as would have been told by refugees after the Second World War. She also viciously attacked Professor Luciuk personally.

Former Ambassador Martin Collacott rose to his defence in a letter to the editor. "She [Neuwirth] takes issue but an examination of the facts makes it clear that it is Neuwirth, and not Luciuk, who is guilty of distortion ....

"She points out that our acceptance rate is 45 to 56 percent (it is actually closer to 60 percent when abandoned and withdrawn claims are not included.) What she neglects to add is that the average for other countries is only around 13 percent since, unlike Canada, they consider that the vast majority of claimants are not genuine refugees. Luciuk's assertion that claimants frequently present concocted stories to the Immigration and Refugee Board is by no means the first time such charges have been made. In 1992, the current Federal Minister of the Environment, David Anderson, who had recently served on the Immigration Appeals Board (predecessor of the Immigration and Refugee Board), was quoted as stating that 'the system is corrupt and the immigration board has become a wretched monster that's out of control.'"

"Compassion fatigue? Perjury fatigue is more like it because they have seen the rule of law perverted so often," he said. "Clearly something is wrong. Either everyone else in the world is wrong or we are out of line, and I think it's us. My own experience as a former Canadian ambassador in Asia and the Middle East led me to the same conclusions. We were told by people how they had succeeded in lying their way through our refugee determination system. Their candor seemed to be based on the assumption that Canadians could not have been stupid enough to set up a system that could be so easily and so thoroughly exploited, and that we must have devised it in order to attract people to Canada who were clever enough to cheat. We were regarded as an international joke in this regard and almost certainly still are. Canada badly needs an informed national debate on both immigration and refugee policy so that the public is fully aware of all the facts."

Next, the Chairman of the Immigration and Refugee Board, Peter Showler, took his licks at Professor Luciuk's piece.

"I have grave concern that he has called into question the integrity of Canada's system and suggested claimants play a game of lies," he wrote, adding this was misleading and inaccurate. "Simply put, our decisions must be efficient, fair and in accordance with the law—all this while under intense scrutiny by the media, the public and the reviewing courts. Our training programs for decision makers, our widely recognized expertise, our thorough documentation and research about conditions in claimants' homelands are considered among the best in the world. Refugee claimants are carefully questioned during a full quasi-judicial hearing. Their credibility and identity are carefully scrutinized. Forensic evidence regarding identity documents is sought as required. This careful scrutiny is crucial and forms the basis of informed and well-reasoned decisions.

"The IRB [Board] will continue to make fair decisions based on the evidence and the law. In doing so, the IRB fulfils Canada's international commitment to providing protection to genuine refugees and contributes to the safety of Canadians."

Next to rise to the occasion was James Bissett, former Executive Director of Canadian Immigration Services.

"Let us not forget something that Mr. Showler fails to mention: all board members are appointed by the government of the day. While some appointees have experience in dealing with refugees, the majority are there as pure patronage.

"Former board member Lubomyr Luciuk has quite properly challenged the integrity and effectiveness of the board. He is not alone. In 1997, a high-level consultative group recommended that the Board be replaced by career public servants specialized in refugee matters. Unfortunately, it is unlikely any government would want to do away with this patronage pork-barrel. Nice try, Mr. Showler, but I'm afraid Mr. Luciuk's concerns are right on."

Professor Luciuk agrees that the board itself should be replaced. Decisions should be made by legal professionals, experts in the field, as is the case in other countries. Instead, the lion's share of board members are not qualified as legal professionals (only 10 percent can be lawyers under the rules) and training is minimal, just two weeks. The place is riddled with politics, hardly surprising given the fact that all are patronage appointees. And the process is inadequate. The only research done when it comes to evaluating claims is internal. This consists of country information, the sworn statement of the claimant, and other pertinent background information. Media searches, witnesses, or even information from Canadian embassy officials in countries abroad, cannot be used as a basis for making decisions, he said.

"The Refugee Claims Officer prepares the package of information and organizes the hearing but cannot cross-examine. I can question but not confront.

"The board isn't representative of Canadian society, which is what it was supposed to be. It's fine to say that it should be comprised 50-50 of females and males because that's the way our society is. But 40 percent to 50 percent of board members are visible minorities. And that's way out of line," he said.

After some run-ins with administrators over this situation, Professor Luciuk was told he could not sit in judgment of any Eastern European claimants, even though he spoke the languages and was an expert on the region. Meanwhile, board members from visible minority ethnic groups were automatically assigned to hearings involving their own ethnic group. White and male, he was also accused of being anti-Semitic by a colleague within weeks of starting work there over a remark he made in the staff room. "I said I was going to Jew's office. Tessie Jew was my supervisor, who was from the Philippines. But this was blown up into a big deal," he said. "My parents were refugees. I spent time in refugee camps. The fact my parents were refugees shaped my life. This experience has been very upsetting to me.

"There is not enough training so this is a learn-on-the-job thing. Beginners are paired with an experienced board member initially. Some are better than others. They weren't all bad but the worst members were the [ethnic] community leaders. They had a political agenda. They were historically inaccurate and politically skewered," he said. "Then there were those who had been refugee lawyers. I'm told these are not lawyers from the top end of the bar. They were a problem."

Pressure to work through the backlog in the Toronto office was always there, and positive decisions were less work than negative ones. That was because a "no" had to be defended in writing with legal reasons because appeals were a certainty. These are difficult for board members who are novices at legalities. "An appeal hinges on a misplaced word," said the professor. "So many don't issue negative opinions because they don't want to write it up or give the person the benefit of the doubt."

The whole exercise is pointless, he believes, because "they all get in. Even if they are given a negative decision, they disappear, change their identity, and reapply. Certain countries are treated better than others. People from mainland China are not deported. In 10 years how many have been deported to China? We never send them back even though there is obvious collusion and corruption with snakeheads to get them in here. These people owe US$25,000 or more to these smugglers, and they are indentured slaves 'til they pay the money off. It is rare that people are genuinely fleeing religious or political persecution."

Consultants would feed groups the same story to tell at the border when they arrived in Canada or on their application, if they claimed refugee status while here on a visa or illegally. "We had a bunch who said that they were persecuted as a result of China's one-child birth control policy. Then everyone became a Christian in China for a while and subject to persecution. Now it would be the Falun Dafa [a religious sect] membership," he said.

Such statements cannot be challenged, but sometimes the claimants, if they are lying, slip up. Professor Luciuk remembered a case involving a Chilean woman who claimed to need refuge from prosecution there because she was the author of an antigovernment political tract. She furnished photocopies of her book. "A smart refugee officer noticed that in her book she forgot to change the ISBN page with the copyright information on it. She had substituted her name on the cover with the real author's name and on the title page but the copyright noted the real author's name," he said. She was refused.

The board members, and hearing results, mostly ignored the details of the United Nations Convention of Refugees, which, for instance, allows rejection of anyone who arrives from a "safe third country" such as the United States. Even though two-thirds of refugee claimants arrive from the U.S. border, they have rarely been denied entry. The Convention also allows rejection of refugee claims if there is a safe place within their country where they can live. "This is the case in Sri Lanka where the Tamils can live in their region. When I pointed this out in a hearing as a result of newspaper reports to that effect, I was advised that such information even though verified was not pertinent," he said.

The professor denied a Mexican gay man's claim on the basis that he may have been discriminated against in his small town for his sexual orientation, but that Mexico's cities were wide open and extremely tolerant of gay life. Another negative decision involved a Chinese woman who claimed to be a devout Roman Catholic in her claim and persecuted as a result. But she could not describe the holy trinity and said that Jesus Christ has a son called Joseph Smith, the founder of the Church of Latter Day Saints, or Mormons. She was not a Roman Catholic.

"Virtually all the claimants were jurisdiction-shopping and they found out that Canada's an easy touch. Real refugees flee immediate danger but always try to stay near their homeland because they really want to return there. I remember one of the few legitimate refugees I came across was a banker from Sudan and his wife. He told us 'I don't want to be a Canadian. I was a man of influence, a banker, then my bitch of a wife got involved in helping black Christians politically. She upset the government, and they took our home and drove us out. Now I'm nothing. The silly woman. I don't want to be here.' When he said that, I knew he was legitimate because a real refugee doesn't want to be a Canadian. He or she wants to go home. In two years at the board he was the only person who said he'd rather be home."

Deportation is virtually voluntary, he said. "If there is no appeal of a negative decision then Immigration sends notice and gives them a certain amount of time to voluntarily remove themselves from the country," he said. "But some people made three claims in three different names in three different cities just to hedge their bets."

Such practices underscored the subjectivity of the process where claimants simply grind down the system until they succeed. "Take the Sikhs. Acceptance rates for them varied greatly in Montreal, Toronto, and Vancouver. Why?

"Canada is an open and generous society, and I went there [the Immigration and Refugee Board] excited about making a contribution and doing important work, and I left disillusioned. My predilection was to say yes," said the professor. "I'm very upset for this country because I don't think liars make good citizens. It has nothing to do with whether these refugees will be hard working or whether they can fill niches and do jobs other Canadians won't accept like cleaning toilet bowls. They may be healthy, hard working, and do jobs Canadians won't do, but we are selling out our citizenship. They are joining our community, and lies don't achieve anything. Being Canadian is like marriage, and you are married to every other Canadian. They lie. They take our money. They bring in Ma and Pa Kettle and all the in-laws and then go back home for vacations. We are exploited by liars who not only benefit from our social safety net but from our legal system. Legal aid is going bust. This just isn't right."

A Refugee Hearing Officer

Elizabeth Dodd is a lawyer who worked in Vancouver for the Immigration and Refugee Board. She felt that the process was a legal sham. She spent hours in 2001 describing to me what goes on there. Her job between 1986 and 1997 was as a Refugee Hearing Officer. Her duties included organizing hearings and preparing documents and research packages for the two-person board members and claimants.

Her tenure overlapped the change in the system in the wake of the controversial *Singh* decision in 1985. The system, until then, consisted of interviews or documentation review at border entry points by trained investigators such as herself. They were empowered to make immediate decisions as to whether to allow people to stay in the country. Rejected persons did not get written reasons explaining the decisions and would be forced to leave immediately. If allowed in, a full-blown hearing before an Immigration Department judge would determine whether they could remain in Canada as long as they needed to.

Then, in 1985, the Supreme Court of Canada ruled that this border-entry interview was unconstitutional, according to the *Charter of Rights and Freedoms*. This was the infamous *Singh* decision. "The court said that an oral hearing, and not merely a paper review, was in order under the *Charter of Rights*," she said. "The old system fell apart in 1985 with the *Singh* decision. Once you get on a plane to Canada that's the beginning of your new life here.

"We pay for them [refugee claimants] to hire lawyers to challenge our laws all the way to the Supreme Court," she said. "I couldn't afford to take a case to the Supreme Court of Canada because it would cost $300,000."

"The situation deteriorated with the new system. The initial Tory appointees were very good in Vancouver. They deferred to Refugee Hearing Officers' information and cross-examination, and 90 percent to 95 percent of decisions were negative. Then the Liberals came in 1993 and kicked out the Tories' well-trained members. After these appointments, all the junk began to arrive—all with the same story and the stories still have not changed. They would go forum shopping. In 1989, most of the Indian claims were turned down in the Vancouver office, so they all began to switch to Calgary where one member always gave a positive outcome. Until two years ago [1999], Algerian claims in Montreal were starting to be rejected. So the 28-year-old males started showing up in Vancouver, with their immigration lawyer, and all requests were expedited in Vancouver and given a yes," she said. "After the Liberals were elected, Refugee Hearing Officers were not allowed to talk to Appeals Officers. This meant that if a refugee claim had been rejected and was appealed we could not share research such as criminal checks or whatever."

Like Professor Luciuk, and other former members of the board, Ms. Dodd said claims were overwhelmingly bogus. "I never, ever saw anyone who met the definition of a refugee in a hearing room. I wrecked their credibility in every single case. These people are just plain liars. I'm not antirefugee or anti-immigrant. But we keep out an American businessman who had a possession charge 25 years before, or if he was caught impaired years ago while driving. We put those people back on planes. But others can come on in anytime they want and tell us anything they want to tell us. These were economic migrants and criminal migrants on the move. Let's face it, a freedom fighter would stay at home despite persecution. These were mostly 28-year-old males taking advantage of the situation."

Sheer volume led to dangerous shortcuts. As these "champagne refugees" poured off planes at the Vancouver Airport daily, and at the U.S. border, the sworn statements taken under oath with a translator at the point of entry were no longer used during the hearing process. "It was too time consuming, we were told," she said.

She told some interesting stories about the 45,000 Iranians, living in Vancouver, who began arriving as refugees after the Shah's reign ended in the late 1970s. "We called them the lipstick and littering cases. Most of the men said they were persecuted for being homosexuals or for distributing pamphlets. Half of them came in from the U.S., where they had been refused entry as refugees. They should have been refused at the border because it was a safe third country. But they weren't. We let everybody in. We even let in a guy who had White-Out on his passport to cover up information. Many of them were rich. They would arrive, I'd examine the contents of their luggage, with white tennis gear, gold jewellery, and asking me what was the best tennis club to join."

Ms Dodd also questions why refugee hearings have to be held *in camera*. "Who is this designed to protect? The board members from criticism. There is no public interest served by keeping the press out of the hearing room. In fact the opposite is true. Ministerial attendance and review was supposed to look after the public interest. But that rarely happened."

Like Toronto and Montreal, Vancouver had its share of South Americans seeking refuge because they were homosexual, Chinese women because they could only have one kid back home, Jehovah's Witnesses from everywhere, Israeli mobsters, Russian Mafioso, or women frightened of getting beaten by their husbands. Some stories would be funny, if the consequences were not so serious. Ms. Dodd said an African claimant refused to give his name, but, when pressed to do so at his refugee hearing, he looked at his lap and the gum wrapper that he was fondling and said his name was "Bubblicious."

An Advisor, Immigration Officer, and Politician

Mike Prue worked as an Immigration officer and ministerial advisor for 14 years, then left in disgust. He ran as a New Democratic candidate in provincial elections and finally became Mayor of East York and, after amalgamation of the area municipalities, a Toronto City Councillor. In 1999, he talked to me about some of his experiences and bemoaned the fact that Canada has become the "laughingstock of the world" when it comes to our open-door refugee policy.

"For 14 years, [until 1992] I was an appeals officer and counselor to the minister [of immigration]," he said. "Canada is a sieve. Canada's refugee system is a joke."

Mr. Prue's biggest nightmare occurred in the early 1990s, when he helped get a violent Jamaican immigrant deported. He also helped beat off an appeal against the deportation of the man, who had multiple convictions already. "The deportation order was upheld, and he was detained for two weeks. The file went to another officer, and the next thing I knew he was on the front page of the newspaper. He had just shot and murdered a Toronto cop," he said. "Every seven days there is a review of those in detention, and the judge said there was no danger. In the 1970s, when you deported someone, they left."

The same incompetence has continued. In 1999, there were 5,000 outstanding deportation orders; by 2001, there were 27,000. Mr. Prue said Canada's international reputation is tarnished. At an international forum he attended in the early 1990s, a paper was circulated with the percentage of refugees allowed in on a country-by-country basis. "The U.S. had 4 percent acceptance, Mexico 3 percent, the U.K. 7 percent, Holland was at 12 percent, and Canada was 84 percent," he recalled. "Somebody stood up and said, 'This must be a typographical error.' Our Canadian representative stood up and said no, the figure was 84 percent, and the whole room broke up into laughter."

Of the 25,000 who claimed to be refugees each year throughout the 1990s, few are, he said, because there is no research done into backgrounds.

"Canada is the only country on Earth that does not have an adversarial system when it comes to determining the validity of a refugee application," he pointed out. "For instance, there were tens of thousands of Portuguese 'refugees' who claim they were discriminated against and wanted refugee status because they were Jehovah's Witnesses," said Prue. "The official church in Portugal said there were less than 1,000 Jehovah's Witnesses in Portugal and they were all accounted for in church records. Even so, Canada processed these tiresome, and fraudulent, applications."

"Nonsense developed," he added. "We also let all the Sri Lankans and Somalians in and shouldn't have. The Guatemalans and Hondurans make their way to Mexico. Mexico rules 3 percent to 5 percent of them as *bona fide* refugees and lets them stay until the political situation in their countries changes. Those that don't convince Mexican authorities they are legitimate refugees get to Tijuana, then escape across the border illegally, go to Canada, and get in. We get the marginal. We get the Guatemalans and Hondurans the Mexicans and Americans won't accept because they are not refugees," he said. "Even China, we let 70 percent in. The refugee criteria here are considered bizarre by the rest of the world. If you call the police and say you are beaten up or because you can't have a second kid you can get into Canada. There is no test of credibility."

"Because we weren't allowed to take fingerprints [for identification], there was a guy in a Swiss jail for heroin and cocaine smuggling. He was in jail and in the meantime his wife claimed refugee status. She was allowed to stay. And via a ministerial order in Canada the husband was allowed to come here and stay because it was ruled he was not to be separated from the family."

Mr. Prue related another horror story about inept judges. A Polish woman came with her husband to Toronto on a visitor's visa in the 1980s and had a baby. Poland was hardly a country gripped by tyranny anymore, but even so the couple applied for refugee status. They got legal aid and a taxpayer-supported lawyer to argue that, because they had a Canadian-born kid, the child had a "charter right" not to be separated from its parents should they be deported. "The refugee board allowed her to stay, and afterward I questioned one of the members as to why the decision was made and he said, 'She had the best pair of legs I have ever seen,'" recalled Prue.

Another refugee, who lost an attempt to become a refugee, appealed in 2002 before a Federal Court and testified that one of the two board members slept throughout her presentation.

Some Thoughts

There is no way of knowing how many "bad apples" we have let into Canada over the years. But we do know that nobody is committed to getting rid of them. The costs to society of this immigration are unknown, in both monetary terms as well as human terms. How many lives are ruined as a result of violence by outsiders? Pockets picked? Seniors shaken down? Teens hooked on heroin? Women raped? Children unsupported by dead-beat dads? Banks robbed, and companies or governments defrauded? Most importantly, why should we put up with anyone from elsewhere who commits a serious crime?

Proposed Solutions

"As soon as your toe touches Canada, the argument is that you are protected by the Charter. And then you fall into an extraordinary stream of judicial recourses that appear to go on forever. Look at the fight we had to put up with to amend the Immigration Act to provide for new proceedings to try and expedite matters. We have to look at the entire question of striking a balance between fair access to the judicial system and inviting abuse."
—Prime Minister Brian Mulroney on July 7, 1991

Nothing has changed. In fact, Mr. Mulroney contributed to the problem. The devastating *Singh* decision occurred in 1985, on Mulroney's watch, and his government's preoccupation, as he stated to me in the above interview, was simply to expedite the refugee determination process. His government also hiked immigration targets to unprecedented levels, without shoring up the system's integrity. The Liberals made matters worse by reducing immigration staff through budget cuts.

Politics has always stood in the way of a solution. The Liberals trot out motherhood statements about how immigrants built the country and unsupported statements that immigrants make a huge contribution. Critics are automatically discounted as "rednecks," so they back off. But even the Liberals have internal polls that show that the vast majority of Canadians want reduced immigration levels and higher-quality people. But the Liberals persist in these policies because the pro-immigrant bloc represents a swing vote that is significant in half of the country's ridings.

I, for one, don't believe that any comprehensive cost-benefit analysis has been done. The report I saw, as described in Section 2, was filled with holes and tracked only limited information by cross-referencing Social Insurance Numbers with federal programs or tax returns. Unquantified were all the "soft" costs such as health care, education, housing, legal aid, pensions, grants, law enforcement, courts, prisons, costs, and damages incurred by victims of immigrant/refugee crimes as well as the huge administrative burden. Without a document that clearly proves that immigration and refugee policies are in the best interests of Canada, there is absolutely no justification for current practices.

The only improvements have been that the federal government—while denying problems exist—has been gradually tweaking the system, plugging holes here and there and taking action when I, or others, expose outright negligence. Another hopeful sign was that Ottawa was truly embarrassed by the Millennium Bomber incident in 1999, and then was raked over the coals, with border sanctions threatened by Washington after the September 11 terrorist attack. This had nothing to do with any direct Canadian link to the case but it was because absolutely nothing had changed in two years.

All that aside, and in the interests of a public debate that I am not optimistic will ever take place in this country, I will propose some changes to our damaging immigration and refugee policy. They address my answers to the four fundamental immigration questions: How many people should we let in? Who should get in? How much humanitarian immigration should be allowed? and Have government procedures met objectives?

Most of my proposed solutions are self-explanatory. I believe they would go a long way toward solving the country's labor needs, meeting our humanitarian obligations, protecting Canadians from criminals, and thus paving the way for an ethical, but more prosperous, future.

1. Any newcomers should be given only probationary status for five years and should waive the right at the point of entry to appeal immediate deportation if they are convicted of any serious crime. They must be removed to the last country they were in before entering Canada, whether that country agrees or not. Sanctions should be imposed on countries that won't cooperate.

2. The current 27,000 deportation orders outstanding should be executed as a matter of national priority and to demonstrate zero tolerance for misdeeds by strangers.

3. Immigration targets should be reduced from 250,000 per year to the replacement level of 80,000 annually and should mainly be "economic" immigrants who meet labor market needs. Demographic arguments that we need large-scale numbers are wrong and the cities that immigrants go to—Toronto, Vancouver, and Montreal—simply cannot afford to assimilate another two million uneducated and unskilled people. (In June 2002, new Immigration minister Denis Coderre announced that he will require immigrants to go to small towns, not the cities, in the future, by making them sign a promise. But this will be challenged in courts or will be ignored, then not enforced.)

4. Immigration, labor, and employment should be merged into a single ministry, and targets fluctuated based on enhancing the creation of wealth. The department should also be co-managed with the Quebec, B.C., and Ontario governments.

5. Canadian citizenship should not be sold to investor or entrepreneur immigrants and should, because of the huge entitlements citizens enjoy, be offered only to those who have lived at least 10 years in the country without committing a crime. Applicants should have to prove, through

tax returns and passport documentation, that they have fulfilled residency requirements and made an economic contribution to the country. No one should be a Canadian for at least 10 years, and he or she should also pass an exam about values, history, and economics.

6. Babies born in Canada to visitors should not be entitled to citizenship unless it is proven that at least one parent is a citizen.

7. A follow-up, by independent consultants, should be undertaken to determine whether business immigrants kept their promises. Those who did not should be fined, deported along with their dependants, and sued for any entitlements they received while defrauding our country.

8. Family reunification should be restricted to wives and dependent children under 18. Sponsors should be responsible for 10 years for supporting them and should also be required to buy private-sector health insurance for 10 years to cover their medical costs. They should not be allowed to enter Canada unless they post a bond sufficient to send their loved ones back home if they cannot financially support them.

9. Canada must change its refugee policy by dismantling its in-country determination system and entertaining applications only from abroad. But first the *Singh* decision, which grants everyone who arrives in Canada *Charter* rights if they want to get involved in the determination process, must be overcome. Current options are to mount another court challenge (which may fail), to overturn the *Singh* decision by invoking the notwithstanding clause (which is impossible because it would take political will), or to amend the *Constitution* (which is unlikely to happen in Canada.)

   The real solution is for Canada to withdraw its signature from the United Nations Convention on Refugees and to sign a side agreement pledging assistance. Free from its rules, Canada could devise a policy that would rescue real refugees, i.e., by recruiting people who are currently in *bona fide* refugee camps abroad.

10. If these actions are not taken, then Ottawa should protect the public. It must triple or quadruple costs by boosting its staff in order to detain all refugee claimants until their identities and backgrounds can be properly checked. Claimants must also be detained until they are medically and psychiatrically examined.

The Immigration and Refugee Board should be closed. Border interviews should be conducted by professionals, and rejects should be put in detention until a proper hearing conducted by professionals, not patronage appointees. Such hearings should permit witnesses, cross-examination, and investigation in order to properly determine the claim's validity.

There should be more than just a probability that the claimant will be persecuted back home, and anyone caught lying, impersonating, or withholding information should be sent immediately back to wherever they came from.

11. Canada should adopt the European system. All of the European countries have the "safe third country" concept and quickly return anyone arriving from a country that is a UN signator, is democratic, follows the rule of law, and has a good human rights record. Germany has a list of countries that are considered safe, and the list is long.

12. Anyone arriving by plane without documents should be sent back on that airline immediately and the company fined. Anyone arriving from the United States as a refugee claimant must be refused because he or she is already in a safe third country. (This change was to be implimented in 2002 but will be challenged or ignored.)

13. "Frivolous claimants," whose information is contradictory or ridiculous, should be expeditiously deported, as should those who make "abusive claims"—people who arrive without documents or with fraudulent documents and do not cooperate.

14. Canada should negotiate, as has Europe, readmission agreements with countries to force them to accept deported persons. If they refuse, any

aid should be cut off, trade privileges denied, and strict visas imposed to stop Canadian tourism to their countries.

15. Any refugee whose claim is under appeal should be removed pending the appeal and should be allowed to return only if successful.

16. The Americans don't give social assistance to refugee claimants and don't allow them to work for six months. After that law was introduced, the percentage of claims dropped 40 percent. Canada should adopt the same rule.

17. Ottawa must properly manage its immigration employees at home and abroad. Creation of an independent investigative unit, to set up stings and other pro-active procedures, must be put in place to end excessive malfeasance. At missions abroad, all visa and other officials should be Canadian, not locals, because Canadians are less likely to be bribed, threatened, or to indulge in nepotism.

18. Visa fees should be increased to pay for a database that will track visa holders' whereabouts. Educational institutions, employers, or relatives who are put down as references on visa applications should be held responsible for ensuring, and proving, that these people have returned home after expiry.

19. All persons calling themselves, or collecting fees as, "immigration consultants" should be registered by the government, monitored, and disciplined. This will end the practice of exploitation that has taken place in the past and the proliferation of sleazy practitioners who coach their clients in ways to defraud or manipulate the system.

20. Canada needs one national identity card for everyone and a national computer system linking all government entitlement programs. The card would contain fingerprints, a photo, date of birth, name, and a microchip full of information. That will give Ottawa a tool to audit the true cost of immigration on an ongoing basis.

21. Canada must stop giving refugee protection to fugitives and stop opposing extradition requests because of capital punishment or other

sentencing practices. To frustrate extradition for any reason other than the merits of the case is an extraterritorial version of obstruction of justice.

22. Medical screening must be done abroad by approved doctors only.

23. Refugees should not be let into the country unless they have a clean bill of health. They must be examined and tested first.

24. Ottawa must stop creeping credentialism. Canada has allowed thousands of doctors, medical professionals, teachers, and others into the country, but their credentials are not recognized by Canada's professional organizations. Even European or American-trained doctors are not licensed to practise medicine here automatically, as Canadian-trained physicians are in their countries. Not only should Ottawa disallow such protectionist practices, but it also should bear the cost of examinations and internships to assimilate foreigners into these fields, which face severe shortages. It's unacceptable, for instance, that one German-trained anaesthetist I interviewed said she had to clean houses for two years because she was unable to qualify for an internship. She eventually left for a position in a British hospital.

Conclusion

Canadians simply cannot afford to continue the government's existing immigration and refugee systems. We cannot afford to stray from the smart economics that dictated previous policies, especially when we have unemployed workers to look after. We cannot allow persons to come into our economy and society without the education and skills to pull their own weight, particularly in a welfare state as generous as ours. We cannot let anyone in without proper screening, and we cannot afford the continuing corruption of our embassies and high commission operations abroad. And once undesirables have been mistakenly allowed in, we must quickly expel them after conviction, before they do more harm. Immigration has never been conducted in such a slipshod and reckless manner as in the last 17 years. It can be blamed, in large measure, for Canada's declining economic performance and will, inevitably, prove ruinous.

Index